W9-BKC-868

For: _____

"For I know the plans I have for you," declares the LORD, "plans to prosper you and not to harm you, plans to give you hope and a future."

Jeremiah 29:11

From: _____

God's Words of Life from The New Student Bible
Copyright © 1998 by Zondervan Publishing House
ISBN 0-310-97185-3

Excerpts taken from:
The New Student Bible
Copyright © 1997 by Zondervan Publishing House,
a division of HarperCollins Publishers.
All rights reserved.

All Scripture quotations, unless otherwise noted, are
taken from the *Holy Bible: New International Version*,
(North American Edition). Copyright © 1973, 1978,
1984, by International Bible Society. Used by permission
of Zondervan Publishing House. All rights reserved. The
"NIV" and "New International Version" trademarks are
registered in th United States Patent and Trademark
Office by International Bible Society.

All right reserved. No part of this publication may be
reproduced, stored in a retrieval system, or transmitted in
any form or by any means—electronic, mechanical, pho-
tocopy, recording, or any other—except for brief quotations in printed reviews, without the prior permission of
the publisher.

Requests for information should be addressed to:

☗ ZondervanPublishingHouse
Mail Drop B20
Grand Rapids, Michigan 49530
http://www.zondervan.com

Senior Editor: Joy Marple
Project Editor: Robin Schmitt
Designer: Patti Matthews

Printed in China

98 99 00 /HK/ 3 2

God's Words
of Life
from
THE NEW
STUDENT BIBLE

Zondervan*Gifts*

We have a gift for inspiration™

God's Words of Life On

God's Words of Life on
ADVERSITY

Jesus taught them saying, "Blessed are those who are persecuted because of righteousness, for theirs is the kingdom of heaven. Blessed are you when people insult you, persecute you and falsely say all kinds of evil against you because of me. Rejoice and be glad, because great is your reward in heaven, for in the same way they persecuted the prophets who were before you."

Matthew 5:10–12

Be strong in the Lord and in his mighty power.

Ephesians 6:10

Have I not commanded you? Be strong and courageous. Do not be terrified; do not be discouraged, for the LORD your God will be with you wherever you go.

Joshua 1:9

David also said to Solomon his son, "Be strong and courageous, and do the work. Do not be afraid or discouraged, for the LORD God, my God, is with you. He will not fail you or forsake you."

1 Chronicles 28:20

I lift up my eyes to the hills— where does my help come from? My help comes from the

God's Words of Life on
ADVERSITY

LORD, the Maker of heaven and earth. He will not let your foot slip— he who watches over you will not slumber; indeed, he who watches over Israel will neither slumber nor sleep. The LORD watches over you— the LORD is your shade at your right hand; the sun will not harm you by day, nor the moon by night. The LORD will keep you from all harm— he will watch over your life; the LORD will watch over your coming and going both now and forevermore.

Psalm 121

The LORD is my rock, my fortress and my deliverer; my God is my rock, in whom I take refuge. He is my shield and the horn of my salvation, my stronghold.

Psalm 18:2

Let us fix our eyes on Jesus, the author and perfecter of our faith, who for the joy set before him endured the cross, scorning its shame, and sat down at the right hand of the throne of God. Consider him who endured such opposition from sinful men, so that you will not grow weary and lose heart.

Hebrews 12:2–3

If God is for us, who can be against us? He who did not spare his own Son, but gave him

7

ADVERSITY

up for us all—how will he not also, along with him, graciously give us all things? Who will bring any charge against those whom God has chosen? It is God who justifies. Who is he that condemns? Christ Jesus, who died—more than that, who was raised to life—is at the right hand of God and is also interceding for us.

Romans 8:31-34

When Sanballat, Tobiah, the Arabs, the Ammonites and the men of Ashdod heard that the repairs to Jerusalem's walls had gone ahead and that the gaps were being closed, they were very angry. They all plotted together to come and fight against Jerusalem and stir up trouble against it. But we prayed to our God and posted a guard day and night to meet this threat.

Nehemiah 4:7–9

Nehemiah 4:9—Praise the Lord and Fight

Nehemiah felt no difficulty combining prayer and action, as this verse shows. Verse 14 gives another unembarrassed combination of spiritual and military tactics: "Remember the Lord and fight."

Devotional Thought on
ADVERSITY

Jesus Christ faced peer pressure from the time he could walk. When he was young, his parents questioned his staying behind to teach in the temple. Later in his life, the religious leaders pressured him to change his message, even threatening him with death. (That's what I call real *peer pressure*!) In the wilderness, Satan himself pressured Jesus to use his power to meet his own needs. Finally, as he was dying on the cross, his peers mocked him and pressured him to come down from the cross if he was really the Christ.

But Jesus had come to do his Father's will, and that principle could not be shaken. He had a purpose in life against which every temptation and pressure was weighed. He was prepared to die to accomplish that purpose.

So don't be discouraged by adversity. The purpose for which God created you is worth the struggle. Keep on trusting him. Keep on living by the principles of love he has written in his Word. Don't give in to peer pressure. Give in to him.

God's Words of Life on
ANGER

The fruit of the Spirit is self-control.

Galatians 5:22–23

"In your anger do not sin:" Do not let the sun go down while you are still angry, and do not give the devil a foothold.

Ephesians 4:26–27

My dear brothers, take note of this: Everyone should be quick to listen, slow to speak and slow to become angry, for man's anger does not bring about the righteous life that God desires.

James 1:19–20

Do not repay anyone evil for evil. Be careful to do what is right in the eyes of everybody. If it is possible, as far as it depends on you, live at peace with everyone. Do not take revenge, my friends, but leave room for God's wrath, for it is written: "It is mine to avenge; I will repay," says the Lord. On the contrary: "If your enemy is hungry, feed him; if he is thirsty, give him something to drink. In doing this, you will heap burning coals on his head." Do not be overcome by evil, but overcome evil with good.

Romans 12:17–21

A man's wisdom gives him patience; it is to his glory to overlook an offense.

Proverbs 19:11

A gentle answer turns away wrath, but a harsh word stirs up anger.

Proverbs 15:1

Jesus replied "You have heard that it was said to the people long ago, 'Do not murder, and anyone who murders will be subject to judgment.' But I tell you that anyone who is angry with his brother will be subject to judgment. Again, anyone who says to his brother, 'Raca,' is answerable to the Sanhedrin. But anyone who says, 'You fool!' will be in danger of the fire of hell. Therefore, if you are offering your gift at the altar and there remember that your brother has something against you, leave your gift there in front of the altar. First go and be reconciled to your brother; then come and offer your gift."

Matthew 5:21–24

Do not be quickly provoked in your spirit, for anger resides in the lap of fools.

Ecclesiastes 7:9

God's Words of Life on
ANGER

Get rid of all bitterness, rage and anger, brawling and slander, along with every form of malice. Be kind and compassionate to one another, forgiving each other, just as in Christ God forgave you.

Ephesians 4:31–32

Starting a quarrel is like breaching a dam; so drop the matter before a dispute breaks out.

Proverbs 17:14

In your anger do not sin; when you are on your beds, search your hearts and be silent.

Psalm 4:4

Psalm 4:4—*Angry Inside*

Is anger sinful? No, though it can certainly lead to sin. This prayer depicts anger springing from anxiety, which proves especially troublesome on sleepless nights. The psalm suggests that, rather than venting your worry in outbursts against others, you should examine your own heart. Paul applied this verse to another situation: difficult personal relationships (Ephesians 4:26).

You're already late to class when that big-eared jock on the wrestling team blind-sides you and sends your books flying.

Your first impulse is to get revenge, if only to yell, "Can't you see where you're going!" You want to stick up for your rights—to save face. But considering the guy's size, you realize you'll probably *lose* face if a fight were to break out.

Regardless of size, James suggests we ought to be "slow to speak and slow to become angry." Mark Twain had a comment on this matter: "When angry, count four; when very angry, swear." Maybe you should instead count to ten or take a couple of deep breaths. The more time you have to think about your response, the less hurtful it will be.

"A gentle answer turns away wrath," wrote Solomon in Proverbs. In other words, be creative in an explosive situation. Adding fuel to a fire just makes a bigger fire. Dealing with people is much the same. You can often diffuse a potentially explosive situation with a touch of humor. For instance, you might try something like: "Hey, roller derby practice doesn't start for another week!"

God's Words of Life on
ANXIETY

Jesus said, "Do not be afraid, little flock."

Luke 12:32

The LORD is my shepherd, I shall not be in want. He makes me lie down in green pastures, he leads me beside quiet waters, he restores my soul. He guides me in paths of righteousness for his name's sake. Even though I walk through the valley of the shadow of death, I will fear no evil, for you are with me; your rod and your staff, they comfort me. You prepare a table before me in the presence of my enemies. You anoint my head with oil; my cup overflows. Surely goodness and love will follow me all the days of my life, and I will dwell in the house of the LORD forever.

Psalm 23

When anxiety was great within me, your consolation O LORD, brought joy to my soul.

Psalm 94:19

"I know the plans I have for you," declares the LORD, "plans to prosper you and not to harm you, plans to give you hope and a future."

Jeremiah 29:11

Cast all your anxiety on Jesus because he cares for you.

1 Peter 5:7

The Lord is near. Do not be anxious about anything, but in everything, by prayer and petition, with thanksgiving, present your requests to God. And the peace of God, which transcends all understanding, will guard your hearts and your minds in Christ Jesus.

Philippians 4:5–7

A righteous man will be remembered forever. He will have no fear of bad news; his heart is steadfast, trusting in the LORD. His heart is secure, he will have no fear.

Psalm 112:6–8

An anxious heart weighs a man down, but a kind word cheers him up.

Proverbs 12:25

Jesus said, "Do not let your hearts be troubled. Trust in God; trust also in me."

John 14:1

Jesus taught them saying, "Do not worry about your life, what you will eat or drink; or about your body, what you will wear. Is not life more important than food, and the body more important than clothes? Look at the birds of the air; they do not sow or reap or store away in barns, and yet your heavenly Father feeds them. Are you not much more valuable than they? The

pagans run after these things and your heavenly
Father knows that you need them. Seek first his
kingdom and his righteousness, and all these
thinkgs will be given to you as well. Therefore,
do not worry about tomorrow, for tomorrow will
worry about itself. Each day has enough trouble
of its own.

Matthew 6:25–34

[God told the Israelites,] "During the forty years
that I led you through the desert, your clothes
did not wear out, nor did the sandals on your
feet. You ate no bread and drank no wine or
other fermented drink. I did this so that you
might know that I am the LORD your God."

Deuteronomy 29:5–6

Deuteronomy 29:5–6—Miracles in the Desert

The Sinai peninsula was a harsh place, and the
Bible records the Israelites' problems with
food and water supplies. But, as these two
verses show, God cared for his people there,
giving them daily food and drink and even
making sure their clothes did not wear out.

Devotional Thought on
ANXIETY

Iread a lot, and every now and then I'll come across something that blasts into my mind with such power that it stays with me for years. That's how I felt when I read the following poem by Elizabeth Cheney, "Overheard in an Orchard":

> Said the Robin to the Sparrow:
> "I should really like to know
> Why these anxious human beings
> Rush about and worry so."
> Said the Sparrow to the Robin:
> "Friend, I think that it must be
> That they have no heavenly Father
> Such as cares for you and me."

When I read that, my first thought was, *Wow—what a profound truth! Even the little birds out in the orchard have more faith than we do. They know God's going to take care of them.*

God *has* promised to meet our needs in the same way he meets the needs of the robin and the sparrow. "And my God will meet all your needs according to his glorious riches in Christ Jesus," the Bible says in Philippians 4:19. We can believe that he will—and relax. Or we can refuse to believe it—and worry. It's up to us.

God's Words of Life on
APPEARANCE

God does not judge by external appearance.

Galatians 2:6

Suppose a man comes into your meeting wearing a gold ring and fine clothes, and a poor man in shabby clothes also comes in. If you show special attention to the man wearing fine clothes and say, "Here's a good seat for you," but say to the poor man, "You stand there" or "Sit on the floor by my feet," have you not discriminated among yourselves and become judges with evil thoughts? Listen, my dear brothers: Has not God chosen those who are poor in the eyes of the world to be rich in faith and to inherit the kingdom he promised those who love him?

James 2:2–5

Jesus replied, "Stop judging by mere appearances, and make a right judgment."

John 7:24

We fix our eyes not on what is seen, but on what is unseen. For what is seen is temporary, but what is unseen is eternal.

2 Corinthians 4:18

Charm is deceptive, and beauty is fleeting; but a woman who fears the LORD is to be praised.

Proverbs 31:30

Jesus taught them saying, "Be careful not to do your 'acts of righteousness' before men, to be seen by them. If you do, you will have no reward from your Father in heaven. So when you give to the needy, do not announce it with trumpets, as the hypocrites do in the synagogues and on the streets, to be honored by men. I tell you the truth, they have received their reward in full. But when you give to the needy, do not let your left hand know what your right hand is doing, so that your giving may be in secret. Then your Father, who sees what is done in secret, will reward you. And when you pray, do not be like the hypocrites, for they love to pray standing in the synagogues and on the street corners to be seen by men. I tell you the truth, they have received their reward in full. But when you pray, go into your room, close the door and pray to your Father, who is unseen. Then your Father, who sees what is done in secret, will reward you."

Matthew 6:1–6

Jesus had no beauty or majesty to attract us to him, nothing in his appearance that we should desire him. He was despised and rejected by men, a man of sorrows, and familiar with suffering. Like one from whom men hide their faces he

19

was despised, and we esteemed him not. Surely he took up our infirmities and carried our sorrows, yet we considered him stricken by God, smitten by him, and afflicted. But he was pierced for our transgressions, he was crushed for our iniquities; the punishment that brought us peace was upon him, and by his wounds we are healed.

Isaiah 53:2–5

Your beauty should not come from outward adornment, such as braided hair and the wearing of gold jewelry and fine clothes. Instead, it should be that of your inner self, the unfading beauty of a gentle and quiet spirit, which is of great worth in God's sight.

1 Peter 3:3–4

God spoke to Samuel- "The LORD does not look at the things man looks at. Man looks at the outward appearance, but the LORD looks at the heart."

1 Samuel 16:7

1 Samuel 16:7—What God Values

What qualified David to be king? Apparently he did not make an overpowering first impression, but God valued hidden qualities far more. Throughout his life David would demonstrate that he loved and trusted God with all his heart, as the law in Deuteronomy 6:4–6 demanded.

Devotional Thought on
APPEARANCE

Almost all of us live two lives: what people see outside and what is really going on inside. In school we learn what outward signs of attention will please the teacher. At a job we learn to "put up a good front" whenever the boss happens to stroll by. As if putting on masks, we style our hair, choose our clothes, and use body language to impress those around us. Over time, we learn to excel at hiding truly serious problems.

In Jesus' day, religious people tried to impress each other with showy outward behavior. They wore gaunt and hungry looks during a brief fast, prayed grandiosely if people were watching, and went so far as to wear Bible verses strapped to their foreheads and left arms.

In his famous Sermon on the Mount, Jesus blasts the hypocrisy behind such seemingly harmless practices. God is not fooled by appearances. We cannot fake behavior to impress him. He knows that inside the best of us lurk dark thoughts of hatred, pride, and lust—internal problems only he can deal with. Jesus goes on to present a truly radical way of life, free of pretense.

God's Words of Life on
ATTITUDE

Jesus replied, "In everything, do to others what you would have them do to you."

Matthew 7:12

Do nothing out of selfish ambition or vain conceit, but in humility consider others better than yourselves. Each of you should look not only to your own interests, but also to the interests of others. Your attitude should be the same as that of Christ Jesus: Who, being in very nature God, did not consider equality with God something to be grasped, but made himself nothing, taking the very nature of a servant, being made in human likeness. And being found in appearance as a man, he humbled himself and became obedient to death— even death on a cross! Therefore God exalted him to the highest place and gave him the name that is above every name, that at the name of Jesus every knee should bow, in heaven and on earth and under the earth, and every tongue confess that Jesus Christ is Lord, to the glory of God the Father.

Philippians 2:3–11

Whatever you do, whether in word or deed, do it all in the name of the Lord Jesus, giving thanks to God the Father through him.

Colossians 3:17

Jesus answered, "When someone invites you to a wedding feast, do not take the place of honor, for a person more distinguished than you may have been invited. If so, the host who invited both of you will come and say to you, 'Give this man your seat.' Then, humiliated, you will have to take the least important place. But when you are invited, take the lowest place, so that when your host comes, he will say to you, 'Friend, move up to a better place.' Then you will be honored in the presence of all your fellow guests. For everyone who exalts himself will be humbled, and he who humbles himself will be exalted."

Luke 14:8–11

Jesus taught them saying, "Be merciful, just as your Father is merciful. Do not judge, and you will not be judged. Do not condemn, and you will not be condemned. Forgive, and you will be forgiven."

Luke 6:36–37

Do not think of yourself more highly than you ought, but rather think of yourself with sober judgment, in accordance with the measure of faith God has given you. Hate what is evil; cling to what is good. Be devoted to one another in brotherly love. Honor one another above

yourselves. Never be lacking in zeal, but keep
your spiritual fervor, serving the Lord. Be joyful
in hope, patient in affliction, faithful in prayer.
Share with God's people who are in need.
Practice hospitality. Bless those who persecute
you; bless and do not curse. Rejoice with
those who rejoice; mourn with those who
mourn. Live in harmony with one another.

Romans 12:3, 9–16

Jesus knew that the Father had put all things
under his power, and that he had come from
God and was returning to God; so he got up
from the meal, took off his outer clothing, and
wrapped a towel around his waist. After that,
he poured water into a basin and began to
wash his disciples' feet, drying them with the
towel that was wrapped around him.

John 13:3–5

John 13:4—The Role of a Servant
Before beginning an intimate meal with his
disciples, Jesus gave them a lesson about
humility. Normally, slaves performed the act of
washing the feet of dinner guests. Here Jesus,
the guest of honor, dressed himself like a
slave, with a towel around his waist, and
insisted on washing the feet of his disciples.

Devotional Thought on
ATTITUDE

When you were with Liz, you were never aware of the long list of things she wasn't or of all the things she couldn't do. You were too busy feeling good and enjoying being around her.

What was it about her that people liked so much? For one thing, she always put the focus on others, never herself. Liz always wanted to know what you'd been doing, how you were feeling, what your plans were.

When you ran into Liz, her smile and her tone of voice said, "I'm so glad to see you!" And you felt that she really meant it.

She was a giver, not a taker. Her interest was in *giving* help, not in demanding it.

Liz's personality was a beautiful form of compensation. If what Liz had to offer the world, instead of physical beauty or athletic skill or brains, was a sweet spirit and a pleasing personality, then that is what she would offer, every day, with all of her might. And people loved her for it.

She could, of course, have taken another path—complaining and moaning that she wasn't more beautiful or richer or more talented. Who'd have wanted to be around her then?

25

God's Words of Life on
CHARACTER

The LORD said to Satan, "Have you considered my servant Job? There is no one on earth like him; he is blameless and upright, a man who fears God and shuns evil. And he still maintains his integrity, though you incited me against him to ruin him without any reason."

Job 2:3

Observe what the LORD your God requires: Walk in his ways, and keep his decrees and commands, his laws and requirements, as written in the Law of Moses, so that you may prosper in all you do and wherever you go.

1 Kings 2:3

Let us purify ourselves from everything that contaminates body and spirit, perfecting holiness out of reverence for God.

2 Corinthians 7:1

As obedient children, do not conform to the evil desires you had when you lived in ignorance. But just as he who called you is holy, so be holy in all you do; for it is written: "Be holy, because I am holy."

1 Peter 1:14–16

God is light; in him there is no darkness at all.

1 John 1:5

Jesus replied, "Be perfect, therefore, as your heavenly Father is perfect."

Matthew 5:48

You are a chosen people, a royal priesthood, a holy nation, a people belonging to God, that you may declare the praises of him who called you out of darkness into his wonderful light.

1 Peter 2:9

You were once darkness, but now you are light in the Lord. Live as children of light.

Ephesians 5:8

LORD, who may dwell in your sanctuary? Who may live on your holy hill? He whose walk is blameless and who does what is rightcous, who speaks the truth from his heart and has no slander on his tongue, who does his neighbor no wrong and casts no slur on his fellowman, who despises a vile man but honors those who fear the LORD, who keeps his oath even when it hurts, who lends his money without usury and does not accept a bribe against the innocent. He who does these things will never be shaken.

Psalm 15

God's Words of Life on
CHARACTER

Therefore, since we have been justified through faith, we have peace with God through our Lord Jesus Christ, through whom we have gained access by faith into this grace in which we now stand. And we rejoice in the hope of the glory of God. Not only so, but we also rejoice in our sufferings, because we know that suffering produces perseverance; perseverance, character; and character, hope. And hope does not disappoint us, because God has poured out his love into our hearts by the Holy Spirit, whom he has given us.

Romans 5:1–5

A truthful witness gives honest testimony, but a false witness tells lies.

Proverbs 12:17

Proverbs 12:17—Deeper Meanings

Some proverbs, disarmingly obvious at first glance, offer deep truth when chewed on. For instance, verse 17 seems to merely repeat the obvious. But its underlying meaning is that a person's character determines his or her actions. You can reflect at length on what this implies about why you do what you do.

Devotional Thought on
CHARACTER

When it comes right down to it, most people are probably uncomfortable with the word "holy." It makes you think of nuns and angels and retired ministers. It's definitely not the label I wanted to be known by.

Maybe that's because my first concern was seldom God—it was *myself*. My self-worth was often defined by how well I was accepted by others. I wanted to fit in. Sure, I was a Christian; I just didn't want to be *too* Christian. As a result, I often compromised my innermost beliefs about what I knew was right and wrong.

By God's standards for our lives, we all fall short. We conform to the pattern of the world when the Bible warns against it. We mimic the lives of unbelievers when we should mirror Christ. In effect, we've turned holiness into a bad word.

"Be holy, because I am holy," the Lord said.

On your own that's as impossible to attain as growing another foot in height. But we're assured in Philippians 2:13 that we're not struggling alone. God is at work in us to *help* us desire and attain his standard and purpose for our lives.

God's Words of Life on
CHOICES

Don't you know that friendship with the world is hatred toward God? Anyone who chooses to be a friend of the world becomes an enemy of God.

James 4:4

As Jesus and his disciples were on their way, he came to a village where a woman named Martha opened her home to him. She had a sister called Mary, who sat at the Lord's feet listening to what he said. But Martha was distracted by all the preparations that had to be made. She came to him and asked, "Lord, don't you care that my sister has left me to do the work by myself? Tell her to help me!" "Martha, Martha," the Lord answered, "you are worried and upset about many things, but only one thing is needed. Mary has chosen what is better, and it will not be taken away from her."

Luke 10:38–42

You were taught, with regard to your former way of life, to put off your old self, which is being corrupted by its deceitful desires; to be made new in the attitude of your minds; and to put on the new self, created to be like God in true righteousness and holiness.

Ephesians 4:22-24

Whether you eat or drink or whatever you do, do it all for the glory of God.

1 Corinthians 10:31

Be clear minded and self-controlled.

1 Peter 4:7

Set your minds on things above, not on earthly things. For you died, and your life is now hidden with Christ in God.

Colossians 3:2–3

The Apostle Paul said, "Everything is permissible for me"—but not everything is beneficial.

1 Corinthians 6:12

If any of you lacks wisdom, he should ask God, who gives generously to all without finding fault, and it will be given to him.

James 1:5

The Spirit of truth will guide you into all truth.

John 16:13

Jesus said, "I have set you an example that you should do as I have done."

John 13:15

God's Words of Life on
CHOICES

By faith Moses, when he had grown up,
refused to be known as the son of Pharaoh's
daughter. He chose to be mistreated along
with the people of God rather than to enjoy
the pleasures of sin for a short time. He
regarded disgrace for the sake of Christ as of
greater value than the treasures of Egypt,
because he was looking ahead to his reward.

Hebrews 11:24-26

Joshua told the Israelites, "If serving the LORD
seems undesirable to you, then choose for
yourselves this day whom you will serve,
whether the gods your forefathers served
beyond the River, or the gods of the Amorites,
in whose land you are living. But as for me and
my household, we will serve the LORD."

Joshua 24:15

Joshua 24:15—Free Choice

After all God had done for them, the Israelites
still faced a fundamental choice. They could
worship the gods their ancestors had served in
Egypt or Mesopotamia, they could follow the
religious practices of the new land they had
entered—or they could follow the God who had
freed them from slavery. Joshua knew exactly
which direction he and his family would take.

During the same week that the youth group has scheduled to host back-to-back Christmas parties for an orphanage and two nursing homes, a non-Christian friend has invited Andy to go snow skiing.

As a leader of his group, Andy feels responsible to be at the youth functions.

And yet, he remembers how much fun he had the only other time he went skiing.

After a lot of prayer and thought, he decided to turn down the invitation.

"When I asked myself, 'What would Jesus do in this situation?' everything became crystal clear."

Perhaps the best way to figure out what Jesus would want you to do is to look at how he made his decisions.

"Jesus gave them this answer: 'I tell you the truth, the Son can do nothing by himself; he can do only what he sees his Father doing, because whatever the Father does the Son also does. For the Father loves the Son and shows him all he does.'" (John 5:19–20).

His secret? Because of his close, moment-by-moment relationship to his heavenly Father (and his commitment to do what was right), Jesus always made the right choices.

Blessed are the peacemakers, for they will be called sons of God.

Matthew 5:9

Do not repay anyone evil for evil. Be careful to do what is right in the eyes of everybody. If it is possible, as far as it depends on you, live at peace with everyone. Do not take revenge, my friends, but leave room for God's wrath, for it is written: "It is mine to avenge; I will repay," says the Lord. On the contrary: "If your enemy is hungry, feed him; if he is thirsty, give him something to drink. In doing this, you will heap burning coals on his head." Do not be overcome by evil, but overcome evil with good.

Romans 12:17–21

Jesus taught them saying, "If your brother sins against you, go and show him his fault, just between the two of you. If he listens to you, you have won your brother over. But if he will not listen, take one or two others along, so that 'every matter may be established by the testimony of two or three witnesses.' If he refuses to listen to them, tell it to the church; and if he refuses to listen even to the church, treat him as you would a pagan or a tax collector."

Matthew 18:15–17

Jesus replied, "Do not judge, or you too will be judged. For in the same way you judge others, you will be judged, and with the measure you use, it will be measured to you. Why do you look at the speck of sawdust in your brother's eye and pay no attention to the plank in your own eye? How can you say to your brother, 'Let me take the speck out of your eye,' when all the time there is a plank in your own eye? You hypocrite, first take the plank out of your own eye, and then you will see clearly to remove the speck from your brother's eye."

Matthew 7:1–5

Jesus said, "You have heard that it was said, 'Eye for eye, and tooth for tooth.' But I tell you, Do not resist an evil person. If someone strikes you on the right cheek, turn to him the other also. And if someone wants to sue you and take your tunic, let him have your cloak as well. If someone forces you to go one mile, go with him two miles."

Matthew 5:38–41

Turn from evil and do good; seek peace and pursue it.

Psalm 34:14

God's Words of Life on
CONFLICT

Consider the blameless, observe the upright; there is a future for the man of peace.

Psalm 37:37

When a man's ways are pleasing to the LORD, he makes even his enemies live at peace with him.

Proverbs 16:7

Jonah prayed to the LORD, "That is why I was so quick to flee to Tarshish. I knew that you are a gracious and compassionate God, slow to anger and abounding in love, a God who relents from sending calamity."

Jonah 4:2

Jonah 4:2—Too Merciful a God?

The poet Robert Frost said, "After Jonah, you could never trust God not to be merciful again." The balky prophet discloses why he ran away from God in the first place: He was afraid God would forgive his archenemies. In fact, God did just that, after Nineveh repented with an eagerness that the Jews themselves often lacked (see Matthew 12:41). Pointedly, the book of Jonah ends with a question. Can anyone put limits on God's mercy and forgiveness?

CONFLICT

Jesus told his followers, "Love your enemies and pray for those who persecute you" (Matthew 5:44). While everyone talks admiringly about that command, loving your enemies is no easy thing. Many people doubt whether it is even right. Should we forgive the Nazis? Should we make a point to be kind to the Ku Klux Klan? Should we have compassion on dictators like Saddam Hussein?

The book of Jonah tells the story of a man whom God instructed to love his enemies in Nineveh. True to life, the prophet Jonah did just the opposite of what God commanded. He refused to go to the people he hated. Instead, he tried to run away from the Lord.

Israelites had reasons to hate and fear Nineveh. But God *loved* Nineveh. He wanted to save the city, not destroy it. He knew Nineveh was ripe for change. When Jonah finally preached there, the entire city believed his message and repented. Though cruel and hardened, Nineveh was ready to believe God. Israel had never responded to a prophet like these Assyrians did.

Jonah needed to develop an attitude like God's toward his enemies. Insistently, God led Jonah to this understanding of his own mind and heart.

CONSCIENCE

Jesus replied, "Your Father sees what is done in secret."

Matthew 6:4

O LORD, you have searched me and you know me. You know when I sit and when I rise; you perceive my thoughts from afar. You discern my going out and my lying down; you are familiar with all my ways. Before a word is on my tongue you know it completely, O LORD. You hem me in—behind and before; you have laid your hand upon me. Such knowledge is too wonderful for me, too lofty for me to attain. Where can I go from your Spirit? Where can I flee from your presence? If I go up to the heavens, you are there; if I make my bed in the depths, you are there. If I rise on the wings of the dawn, if I settle on the far side of the sea, even there your hand will guide me, your right hand will hold me fast. If I say, "Surely the darkness will hide me and the light become night around me," even the darkness will not be dark to you; the night will shine like the day, for darkness is as light to you. Search me, O God, and know my heart; test me and know my anxious thoughts. See if there is any offensive way in me, and lead me in the way everlasting.

Psalm 139:1–12, 23–24

God's Words of Life on
CONSCIENCE

The word of God is living and active. Sharper than any double-edged sword, it penetrates even to dividing soul and spirit, joints and marrow; it judges the thoughts and attitudes of the heart.

Hebrews 4:12

Jesus said, "I will ask the Father, and he will give you another Counselor to be with you forever—the Spirit of truth. When he comes, he will convict the world of guilt in regard to sin."

John 14:16; 16:8

Therefore, brothers, since we have confidence to enter the Most Holy Place by the blood of Jesus, by a new and living way opened for us through the curtain, that is, his body, and since we have a great priest over the house of God, let us draw near to God with a sincere heart in full assurance of faith, having our hearts sprinkled to cleanse us from a guilty conscience.

Hebrews 10:19–22

The Apostle Paul said, "I strive always to keep my conscience clear before God and man."

Acts 24:16

God's Words of Life on
CONSCIENCE

You must no longer live as the Gentiles do, in the futility of their thinking. They are darkened in their understanding and separated from the life of God because of the ignorance that is in them due to the hardening of their hearts. Having lost all sensitivity, they have given themselves over to sensuality so as to indulge in every kind of impurity, with a continual lust for more.

Ephesians 4:17–19

Ephesians 4:19—Loss of Sensitivity

Medical conditions that destroy nerves—leprosy, spinal cord injury, diabetes—are among the most difficult to treat. Without a sense of touch or pain, the patient can get a bedsore by lying in the same position too long, or a footsore by wearing too-tight shoes. The body no longer warns of danger. According to Paul, people can also develop a kind of moral insensitivity, silencing their consciences and hardening their hearts. That condition can prove fatal.

Devotional Thought on
CONSCIENCE

I wrote a letter to a friend but didn't have any postage. So I began peeling an uncanceled stamp from another letter to use again. No *big deal—it's just a stamp*, I thought.

Later that day I was nearly to the post office when I noticed I was driving ten miles per hour over the speed limit. But *everyone is going that fast*, I rationalized.

And I kept the extra dime the postal clerk mistakenly gave me. *It's just small change*, I reasoned.

These were all little wrongs—things that really didn't hurt anyone else. Still, I was amazed how often and easily I minimized them. I had been living as if only the "big" stuff—the *real grossies*—mattered, and had developed a callousness toward small infractions.

I can't say my life has changed drastically since that realization hit. And yet I find myself being a little more literal about right and wrong. I weigh my small decisions more carefully, knowing that will help me with big decisions.

Each day has become an experiment in which I, like Paul, strive to keep my conscience clear before God and man.

God's Words of Life on
CONSEQUENCES

The LORD God commanded the man, "You are free to eat from any tree in the garden; but you must not eat from the tree of the knowledge of good and evil, for when you eat of it you will surely die."

Genesis 2:16–17

Do not be deceived: God cannot be mocked. A man reaps what he sows. The one who sows to please his sinful nature, from that nature will reap destruction; the one who sows to please the Spirit, from the Spirit will reap eternal life.

Galatians 6:7–8

The wages of sin is death, but the gift of God is eternal life in Christ Jesus our Lord.

Romans 6:23

When the Son of Man comes in his glory, and all the angels with him, he will sit on his throne in heavenly glory. All the nations will be gathered before him, and he will separate the people one from another as a shepherd separates the sheep from the goats. He will put the sheep on his right and the goats on his left. Then the King will say to those on his right, "Come, you who are blessed by my Father; take your inheri-

CONSEQUENCES

tance, the kingdom prepared for you since the creation of the world. For I was hungry and you gave me something to eat, I was thirsty and you gave me something to drink, I was a stranger and you invited me in, I needed clothes and you clothed me, I was sick and you looked after me, I was in prison and you came to visit me." Whatever you did for one of the least of these brothers of mine, you did for me." Then he will say to those on his left, "Depart from me, you who are cursed, into the eternal fire prepared for the devil and his angels. For I was hungry and you gave me nothing to eat, I was thirsty and you gave me nothing to drink, I was a stranger and you did not invite me in, I needed clothes and you did not clothe me, I was sick and In prison and you did not look after me." Whatever you did not do for one of the least of these, you did not do for me." Then they will go away to eternal punishment, but the righteous to eternal life.

Matthew 25:31–36,40-43,45-46

He who sows wickedness reaps trouble.

Proverbs 22:8

God's Words of Life on
CONSEQUENCES

King David cried, "O my son Absalom! My son, my son Absalom! If only I had died instead of you—O Absalom, my son, my son!"

2 Samuel 18:33

2 Samuel 18:33—Sin As a Cancer

Second Samuel 11–20 reads like a history of a spreading cancer. David caught a glimpse of Bathsheba's beautiful, naked body and impulsively sent for her. The cover-up required a murder. Nobody could deny it was an ugly business: Even David admitted it when Nathan confronted him. However, it was soon over. He repented. He married Bathsheba. He did not intend to fall to that temptation again. But the consequences of the sin were far from over.

Devotional Thought on
CONSEQUENCES

Buried in the shadows of Paul's closet is a large box brimming with cards and letters from his girlfriend Denise. Their love seemed Hallmark perfect until she got pregnant and, against his wishes, had an abortion. And now, the letters have stopped coming.

"The people at the clinic told her abortion was really no big deal—it was just like removing a 'little glob of tissue.' Maybe it's easier to kill something if you think of it like that," Paul said. "But that 'little glob of tissue' had a heartbeat. It was my child. And my child would have been three on October eleventh."

It was difficult listening to Paul because I knew the roots of pain went clear to his bones. I also knew, as did Paul, that the baby never would have been conceived had Paul maintained his relationship with God. But he scrapped his beliefs when Denise entered the picture.

At any point God's forgiveness could be extended to him for the asking. Paul's sins (and Denise's, too) could be erased easily, as they can with any of us. But God's forgiveness doesn't always erase the consequences of sin. Paul's lonely, very painful thoughts about his child are proof of that.

God's Words of Life on
DATING & MARRIAGE

The LORD God caused the man to fall into a deep sleep; and while he was sleeping, he took one of the man's ribs and closed up the place with flesh. Then the LORD God made a woman from the rib he had taken out of the man, and he brought her to the man. The man said, "This is now bone of my bones and flesh of my flesh; she shall be called 'woman,' for she was taken out of man." For this reason a man will leave his father and mother and be united to his wife, and they will become one flesh.

Genesis 2:21–24

Jesus replied, "What God has joined together, let man not separate."

Matthew 19:6

Wives, in the same way be submissive to your husbands so that, if any of them do not believe the word, they may be won over without words by the behavior of their wives, when they see the purity and reverence of your lives. Husbands, in the same way be considerate as you live with your wives, and treat them with respect as the weaker partner and as heirs with you of the gracious gift of life, so that nothing will hinder your prayers.

1 Peter 3:1–2,7

DATING & MARRIAGE

Submit to one another out of reverence for Christ. Wives, submit to your husbands as to the Lord. For the husband is the head of the wife as Christ is the head of the church, his body, of which he is the Savior. Now as the church submits to Christ, so also wives should submit to their husbands in everything. Husbands, love your wives, just as Christ loved the church and gave himself up for her.

Ephesians 5:21–25

A wife of noble character who can find? She is worth far more than rubies. Her husband has full confidence in her and lacks nothing of value. She brings him good, not harm, all the days of her life. She is clothed with strength and dignity. She speaks with wisdom, and faithful instruction is on her tongue. She watches over the affairs of her household and does not eat the bread of idleness. Her children arise and call her blessed; her husband also, and he praises her: "Many women do noble things, but you surpass them all."

Proverbs 31:10-12,25-29

Do not be yoked together with unbelievers. For what do righteousness and wickedness have in common? Or what fellowship can light have with darkness?

2 Corinthians 6:14

Samson went down to Timnah and saw there a young Philistine woman. When he returned, he said to his father and mother, "I have seen a Philistine woman in Timnah; now get her for me as my wife." His father and mother replied, "Isn't there an acceptable woman among your relatives or among all our people? Must you go to the uncircumcised Philistines to get a wife?" But Samson said to his father, "Get her for me. She's the right one for me."

Judges 14:2

Judges 14:2—Samson: A Weakness for Women

Samson, the strongest man of his generation, was tragically unable to control his lust. When he saw an attractive woman, he wanted her. He first fell for a young woman he saw in a Philistine village just across the valley from his home. His parents tried to dissuade him, since her religion and culture were unacceptable, but he would not listen. Desire was his only rule. The marriage ended in a matter of days and resulted in dozens of deaths.

DATING & MARRIAGE

In ancient times women were often viewed as men's property, good for bearing children and not much more. Proverbs, addressed to young men approaching the age of marriage, takes a different view. It holds up marriage as a crucial choice, to be made with great care.

A good wife (or husband, we can assume) will make or break her partner's life. Her duties lay the foundation for her family's welfare (Proverbs 14:1; 31:10–31). She shares with her husband the most significant task of teaching their children the way of wisdom (Proverbs 1:8–9; 6:20). Therefore, her character matters far more than her physical beauty.

Not that Proverbs ignores the physical side of love. It urges marriage partners to rejoice in their love, to be captivated by it (Proverbs 5:18–19). It warns young people against sexual sin precisely because this wastes sexuality on unsatisfying, unloving relationships. Sex ought to be saved for the long-lasting, productive joy of marriage.

God's Words of Life on
ENCOURAGEMENT

Encourage one another and build each other up.

1 Timothy 5:11

For everthing that was written in the past was written to teach us, so that through endurance and the encouragement of the Scriptures we might have hope.

Romans 15:4

Strengthen the feeble hands, steady the knees that give way; say to those with fearful hearts, "Be strong, do not fear; your God will come, he will come with vengeance; with divine retribution he will come to save you." Then will the eyes of the blind be opened and the ears of the deaf unstopped. Then will the lame leap like a deer, and the mute tongue shout for joy. Water will gush forth in the wilderness and streams in the desert.

Isaiah 35:3–6

May our Lord Jesus Chriat himself and God our Father, who loved us and by his grace gave us eternal encouragement and good hope.

2 Thessalonians 2:16

Encourage one another daily, as long as it is called Today.

Hebrews 3:13

Let us hold unswervingly to the hope we profess, for God who promised is faithful. And let us consider how we may spur one another on toward love and good deeds. Let us not give up meeting together, as some are in the habit of doing, but let us encourage one another—and all the more as you see the Day approaching.

Hebrews 10:23–25

Jesus said, "Where two or three come together in my name, there am I with them."

Matthew 18:20

The Apostle Paul wrote, Whatever was to my profit I now consider loss for the sake of Christ. What is more, I consider everything a loss compared to the surpassing greatness of knowing Christ Jesus my Lord, for whose sake I have lost all things. I want to know Christ and the power of his resurrection and the fellowship of sharing in his sufferings. I press on to take hold of that for which Christ Jesus took hold of me. I do not consider myself yet to have taken hold of it. But one thing I do: Forgetting what is behind and straining toward what is ahead, I press on toward the goal to win the prize for which God has called me heavenward in Christ Jesus.

Philippians 3:7-8,10,12-14

God's Words of Life on
ENCOURAGEMENT

May our Lord Jesus Christ himself and God our Father, who loved us and by his grace gave us eternal encouragement and good hope, encourage your hearts and strengthen you in every good deed and word.

2 Thessalonians 2:16–17

You are no longer foreigners and aliens, but fellow citizens with God's people and members of God's household.

Ephesians 2:19

Ephesians 2:19—For the Discouraged

Ephesians is a rich book that expands the message of Jesus' parable of the Lost Son (Luke 15). A big "Welcome Home!" banner is stretched across the lawn, confetti swirls in the air, balloons lunge skyward, and a band plays. Christians have been adopted directly into the family of God. This is a good news book, to put it mildly. If you feel discouraged or wonder if God really cares or question whether the Christian life is worth the effort, read Ephesians. You will no longer feel like an orphan.

ENCOURAGEMENT

The small band of Jewish exiles built an altar on the grounds of the ruined temple when they returned to Jerusalem. But soon they grew discouraged about the actual rebuilding. They had enough trouble finding shelter and scratching out a living from the land. When their non-Jewish neighbors fought against rebuilding the temple, the former exiles gave up. Their hopes of a glorious "new beginning" began to fade.

The temple stayed in a state of disrepair for nearly 20 years, until the prophets Haggai and Zechariah stirred up renewed interest. These prophets saw that as long as the temple lay in ruins, Israel's distinctive character as a people of God was ruined, too. At their urging, the Jews organized to build again.

The book of Zechariah is a record from that critical period of rebuilding. Its first recorded message dates from approximately two months after the temple foundation was laid. The temple was completed four years later, at least partly due to Zechariah's encouraging words.

The last half of Zechariah widens its view to the whole world. The small refugee community of Jews, Zechariah says, holds the world's future. Their new beginning would become the hope of the world.

God's Words of Life on
ETERNAL LIFE

Jesus said, "I am the resurrection and the life. He who believes in me will live, even though he dies; and whoever lives and believes in me will never die."

John 11:25–26

Jesus answered, "I am the way and the truth and the life. No one comes to the Father except through me."

John 14:6

Jesus said to his disciples, "If anyone would come after me, he must deny himself and take up his cross and follow me. For whoever wants to save his life will lose it, but whoever loses his life for me will find it."

Matthew 16:24–25

Peter told Jesus, "You have the words of eternal life. We believe and know that you are the Holy One of God."

John 6:68

God has given us eternal life, and this life is in his Son. He who has the Son has life; he who does not have the Son of God does not have life. I write these things to you who believe in the name of the Son of God so that you may know that you have eternal life.

1 John 5:11–13

God's Words of Life on
ETERNAL LIFE

Jesus said, "Everyone who has left houses or brothers or sisters or father or mother or children or fields for my sake will receive a hundred times as much and will inherit eternal life."

Matthew 19:29

Now that you have been set free from sin and have become slaves to God, the benefit you reap leads to holiness, and the result is eternal life. For the wages of sin is death, but the gift of God is eternal life in Christ Jesus our Lord.

Romans 6:22–23

Jesus said, "Here I am! I stand at the door and knock. If anyone hears my voice and opens the door, I will come in and eat with him, and he with me."

Revelation 3:20

Now there was a man of the Pharisees named Nicodemus, a member of the Jewish ruling council. He came to Jesus at night and said, "Rabbi, we know you are a teacher who has come from God. For no one could perform the miraculous signs you are doing if God were not with him." In reply Jesus declared, "I tell you the truth, no one can see the kingdom of God unless he is born again."

55

God's Words of Life on
ETERNAL LIFE

"How can a man be born when he is old?" Nicodemus asked. "Surely he cannot enter a second time into his mother's womb to be born!" Jesus answered, "I tell you the truth, no one can enter the kingdom of God unless he is born of water and the Spirit. Flesh gives birth to flesh, but the Spirit gives birth to spirit."

John 3:1–6

My heart is glad and my tongue rejoices; my body also will rest secure, because you will not abandon me to the grave, nor will you let your Holy One see decay. You have made known to me the path of life; you will fill me with joy in your presence, with eternal pleasures at your right hand.

Psalm 16:9–11

Psalm 16:9–11—Resurrection!

In this confident, happy psalm, David rejoices that the life God gives cannot be canceled by the grave. Generally, the Old Testament offers little insight into life after death, but here David's faith carries him to a deeper understanding. The apostles Peter and Paul understood this psalm as prophesying Jesus' resurrection (see Acts 2:25–28; 13:35–37). Because of Jesus' resurrection, David and all God's people would come to new life in him.

Devotional Thought on
ETERNAL LIFE

What happens to you after you die? People have always wanted an answer to that question, and the psalmists were no different.

Israelites called the dark and shadowy place where dead people go "Sheol." When you got there, your life seemed thoroughly finished. The psalmists emphatically did not want to go there, and they asked God, when praying for his help, what possible good there might be in death. Sheol was the great leveler: it meant the end of plans, of worship, of a relationship with God (Psalms 30:9; 88:5; 146:4). The dead were found there, not the living.

Yet some psalms also hint at a happier view. They hold such a strong view of God's authority that they show —vaguely, but unmistakably—God's power over the grave.

What did they expect life after death to be like, if God's power redeemed someone from Sheol? You won't find a clearly defined picture of heaven here—only hints. The psalmists' thoughts center on God's face and his presence. For God is the only unchangeable reality: Wherever you are, in life or in death, he will be there. He is the ultimate reward to those who love him.

God's Words of Life on
FAILURE

Jesus replied, "Watch and pray so that you will not fall into temptation. The spirit is willing, but the body is weak."

Matthew 26:41

Though a righteous man falls seven times, he rises again.

Proverbs 24:16

When I said, "My foot is slipping," your love, O LORD, supported me.

Psalm 94:18

Though I have fallen, I will rise. Though I sit in darkness, the LORD will be my light.

Micah 7:8

Yet this I call to mind and therefore I have hope: Because of the LORD'S great love we are not consumed, for his compassions never fail. The yare new every morning; great is your faithfulness.

Lamentations 3:21-23

Forget the former things; do not dwell on the past.

Isaiah 43:18

If anyone is in Christ, he is a new creation; the old has gone, the new has come!

2 Corinthians 5:17

God's Words of Life on
FAILURE

I waited patiently for the LORD; he turned to me
and heard my cry. He lifted me out of the slimy
pit, out of the mud and mire; he set my feet on a
rock and gave me a firm place to stand.

Psalm 40:1

Forgetting what is behind and straining toward
what is ahead, I [Paul] press on toward the goal
to win the prize for which God has called me
heavenward in Christ Jesus.

Philippians 3:13–14

Seizing Jesus, they led him away and took him
into the house of the high priest Peter followed
at a distance. But when they had kindled a fire in
the middle of the courtyard and had sat down
together, Peter sat down with them. A servant girl
saw him seated there in the firelight. She looked
closely at him and said, "This man was with him."
But he denied it. "Woman, I don't know him," he
said. A little later someone else saw him and
said, "You also are one of them." "Man, I am not!"
Peter replied. About an hour later another assert-
ed, "Certainly this fellow was with him, for he is a
Galilean." Peter replied, "Man, I don't know what
you're talking about!" Just as he was speaking,
the rooster crowed. The Lord turned and looked
straight at Peter Then Peter remembered the
word the Lord had spoken to him: "Before the

rooster crows today, you will disown me three times." And he went outside and wept bitterly.

Luke 22:54–62

When they had finished eating, Jesus said to Simon Peter, "Simon son of John, do you truly love me more than these?" "Yes, Lord," he said, "you know that I love you." Jesus said, "Feed my lambs." Again Jesus said, "Simon son of John, do you truly love me?" He answered, "Yes, Lord, you know that I love you." Jesus said, "Take care of my sheep." The third time he said to him, "Simon son of John, do you love me?" Peter was hurt because Jesus asked him the third time, "Do you love me?" He said, "Lord, you know all things; you know that I love you." Jesus said, "Feed my sheep."

John 21:15–17

John 21:15—Do You Love Me?
John ends his book with a moving scene in which Jesus spoke to Peter and "the disciple whom Jesus loved," presumably John himself. Jesus asked Peter the same question three times, a painful reminder of Peter's three denials of him. But this reinstatement helped embolden Peter to become one of the early church's most fearless spokesmen.

Devotional Thought on
FAILURE

Why is it that sin is so hard to overcome? When Paul was trying to be a good person (by keeping all the law) in his own strength, he was ultimately defeated by the sin problem. Although his intentions were good, he was attempting to win the battle over sin by his own plan and ability. There is only one solution to that kind of struggle. Paul concludes at the end, "What a wretched man I am! Who will rescue me from this body of death? Thanks be to God—through Jesus Christ our Lord!" (Romans 7:24–25).

The very best proof of the Christian faith is a believer with a changed life. Paul calls Christians to "count yourselves dead to sin but alive to God in Christ Jesus" (Romans 6:11), and he wrote as if this were really possible!

Conflict won't disappear completely yet, says Paul, for we are part of a "groaning," imperfect creation (Romans 8:18–25). But with God working for us, we can be *more than* conquerors, and one day God will make all of creation perfect again. That promise should assure us that nothing can separate us from God's love (Romans 8:38–39).

FAITH

Thomas was not with the disciples when Jesus came. So the other disciples told him, "We have seen the Lord!" But he said to them, "Unless I see the nail marks in his hands and put my finger where the nails were, and put my hand into his side, I will not believe it." A week later his disciples were in the house again, and Thomas was with them. Though the doors were locked, Jesus came and stood among them and said, "Peace be with you!" Then he said to Thomas, "Put your finger here; see my hands. Reach out your hand and put it into my side. Stop doubting and believe." Thomas said to him, "My Lord and my God!" Then Jesus told him, "Because you have seen me, you have believed; blessed are those who have not seen and yet have believed."

John 20:24–29

The righteous will live by faith.

Romans 1:17

When Jesus had entered Capernaum, a centurion came to him, asking for help. "Lord," he said, "my servant lies at home paralyzed and in terrible suffering." Jesus said to him, "I will go and heal him." The centurion replied, "Lord, I do not deserve to have you come under my roof. But just say the word, and my servant will be healed. For I myself am a man under authority, with soldiers under me. I tell this one, 'Go,' and he goes;

and that one, 'Come,' and he comes. I say to my servant, 'Do this,' and he does it." When Jesus heard this, he was astonished and said to those following him, "I tell you the truth, I have not found anyone in Israel with such great faith."

Matthew 8:5–10

Jesus called the children to him and said, "Let the little children come to me, and do not hinder them, for the kingdom of God belongs to such as these. I tell you the truth, anyone who will not receive the kingdom of God like a little child will never enter it."

Luke 18:16–17

We live by faith, not by sight.

2 Corinthians 5:7

Without faith it is impossible to please God, because anyone who comes to him must believe that he exists and that he rewards those who earnestly seek him.

Hebrews 11:6

Faith is being sure of what we hope for and certain of what we do not see. Since we are surrounded by such a great cloud of witnesses,let us throw off everything that hinders and the sin that so easily entangles, and let us run with perseverance the race marked out for us. Let us fix our

eyes on Jesus, the author and perfecter of our
faith,who for the joy set before him endured the
cross, scorning its shame, and sat down at the
right hand of the throne of God. Consider him
who endured such opposition from sinful men,
so that you will not grow weary and lose heart.

Hebrews 11:1, 12:1-3

Righteousness from God comes through faith in
Jesus Christ to all who believe.

Romans 3:22

For a little while you may have had to suffer
grief in all kinds of trials. These have come so
that your faith—of greater worth than gold,
which perishes even though refined by fire—
may be proved genuine and may result in praise,
glory and honor when Jesus Christ is revealed.

1 Peter 1:6–7

1 Peter 1:7—Refiner's Fire
A prospector who discovers gold-bearing rock
sends it to an assayer for evaluation. Testing by
fire will melt off most impurities, and the true
gold will emerge purified. Suffering acts in
much the same way, says Peter: It exposes and
refines true faith. In addition, faith in the midst
of such trials will earn future rewards.

Devotional Thought on
FAITH

What are signs of true faith?

The author of Hebrews launches into a detailed description of faith, complete with references to several dozen biographical models. (Some have dubbed Hebrews 11 the "Faith Hall of Fame.") "Without faith," Hebrews says bluntly, "it is impossible to please God" (Hebrews 11:6).

But the picture of faith emerging from these chapters contains some surprises. The author uses words and phrases like "persevere," "endure," "do not lose heart." In many instances, the heroes cited did not receive the promise they hoped for; some ended up flogged and destitute, hiding out in goatskins (Hebrews 11:36–38). Many died horrible deaths.

Faith, concludes the author, most resembles a difficult race. The runner has his or her eyes on the winner's prize, and despite nagging temptations to slacken the pace, refuses to let up until he or she crosses the finish line.

Hebrews holds up Jesus, who endured great suffering for our sakes (Hebrews 12:2–3), as the ultimate example. The faith described in Hebrews is not sugarcoated; God does not guarantee a life of luxury and ease. It is tough faith: a constant commitment to hang on and believe God against all odds, no matter what.

God's Words of Life on
FAMILY RELATIONSHIPS

Each of you should look not only to your own interests, but also to the interests of others.

Philippians 2:4

Above all, love each other deeply, because love covers over a multitude of sins.

1 Peter 4:8

Israel loved Joseph more than any of his other sons, because he had been born to him in his old age; and he made a richly ornamented robe for him. When his brothers saw that their father loved him more than any of them, they hated him and could not speak a kind word to him. Joseph had a dream, and when he told it to his brothers, they hated him all the more. They plotted to kill him. "Here comes that dreamer!" they said to each other. "Come now, let's kill him."

Genesis 37:3–5, 18–20

Genesis 37:19–20—Family Battles
Joseph and his brothers fought bitterly—almost to the death. Nobody, it seems, can fight like brothers and sisters. Their very closeness seems to rub salt in their wounds. Joseph's story is the last of the brotherly quarrels of Genesis.

Devotional Thought on
FAMILY RELATIONSHIPS

If you're a Christian, you definitely have a responsibility to make every effort to resolve conflicts in a peaceful manner and avoid them whenever possible. Here is a suggestion that might help you do that: *Learn to live for others.*

A brother and sister in Seattle, Washington, amazed me with the love they demonstrated for each other. While staying in their home, I was delighted to see the older brother wake his sister in the morning and ask what she would like for breakfast. Instead of the cruel way a brother often treats his sister, he treated her with the kindness that is usually only reserved for a very close friend. She treated him with respect and admiration and proudly told me of his athletic accomplishments. When they each left the house that morning to go their separate ways it was with expressions of love and good luck. Compare that attitude with the fighting that usually rings through a house before school. An unselfish view of life, backed by an all-out effort to care for the other members of your family, can make a miraculous difference in your home.

God's Words of Life on
FORGIVENESS

If we confess our sins, he is faithful and just and will forgive us our sins and purify us from all unrighteousness.

1 John 1:9

The LORD came down in the cloud and stood there with him and proclaimed his name, the LORD. And he passed in front of Moses, proclaiming, "The LORD, the LORD, the compassionate and gracious God, slow to anger, abounding in love and faithfulness, maintaining love to thousands, and forgiving wickedness, rebellion and sin."

Exodus 34:5–7

You are a forgiving God, gracious and compassionate, slow to anger and abounding in love.

Nehemiah 9:17

Peter came to Jesus and asked, "Lord, how many times shall I forgive my brother when he sins against me? Up to seven times?" Jesus answered, "I tell you, not seven times, but seventy-seven times. Therefore, the kingdom of heaven is like a king who wanted to settle accounts with his servants. As he began the settlement, a man who owed him ten thousand talents was brought to him. Since he was not able to pay, the master ordered that he

and his wife and his children and all that he
had be sold to repay the debt. The servant fell
on his knees before him. 'Be patient with me,'
he begged, 'and I will pay back everything.' The
servant's master took pity on him, canceled
the debt and let him go. But when that servant
went out, he found one of his fellow servants
who owed him a hundred denarii. He grabbed
him and began to choke him. 'Pay back what
you owe me!' he demanded. His fellow servant
fell to his knees and begged him, 'Be patient
with me, and I will pay you back.' But he
refused. Instead, he went off and had the man
thrown into prison until he could pay the debt.
When the other servants saw what had happened, they were greatly distressed and went
and told their master everything that had happened. Then the master called the servant in.
'You wicked servant,' he said, 'I canceled all
that debt of yours because you begged me to.
Shouldn't you have had mercy on your fellow
servant just as I had on you?' In anger his master turned him over to the jailers to be tor-
tured, until he should pay back all he owed.
This is how my heavenly Father will treat each
of you unless you forgive your brother from
your heart."

Matthew 18:21–35

God's Words of Life on
FORGIVENESS

If you forgive men when they sin against you, your heavenly Father will also forgive you. But if you do not forgive men their sins, your Father will not forgive your sins.

Matthew 6:14–15

Be merciful, just as your Father is merciful.

Luke 6:36

Bear with each other and forgive whatever grievances you may have against one another. Forgive as the Lord forgave you.

Colossians 3:13

Who is a God like you, who pardons sin and forgives the transgression of the remnant of his inheritance? You do not stay angry forever but delight to show mercy.

Micah 7:18

Micah 7:18—Nobody Like God
Theologians use big words to describe God's unique qualities: transcendence, omnipotence, omnipresence. Micah marveled even more over this: God's forgiveness. Unlike the angry gods of other nations, Israel's God delighted to show mercy.

Devotional Thought on
FORGIVENESS

The so-called "cursing psalms" express the hideousness of violence and injustice. Unless you feel the depth of this, you cannot understand the depth of God's forgiveness, offered freely to anyone who pleads for mercy. God is not merely letting people off on a legal technicality. He hears the cry of their victims, and more: He shares it. In Jesus, God was the victim, beaten, cursed, killed.

The New Testament actually quoted two of the cursing psalms, referring to Judas's betrayal of Jesus These psalms speak of bitter injustice, and Jesus suffered the ultimate injustice. But the final word comes from Jesus himself: "Father, forgive them, for they do not know what they are doing."

If we follow Jesus' example, we dare not mouth the cursing psalms when we think of our enemies. These psalms are not for us to borrow from, as are other psalms. Yet these cursing psalms remind us of the bitter suffering many experience, and reading them can impel us to fight for justice. More, they remind us to forgive. For God, hearing such cries from the victim, having suffered as they suffer, forgives. So can we.

71

God's Words of Life on
FRIENDSHIP

Jonathan became one in spirit with David, and he loved him as himself.

1 Samuel 18:1

A man of many companions may come to ruin, but there is a friend who sticks closer than a brother.

Proverbs 18:24

Two are better than one, because they have a good return for their work: If one falls down, his friend can help him up. But pity the man who falls and has no one to help him up!

Ecclesiastes 4:9–10

As iron sharpens iron, so one man sharpens another.

Proverbs 27:17

Wounds from a friend can be trusted.

Proverbs 27:6

A righteous man is cautious in friendship.

Proverbs 12:26

The pleasantness of one's friend springs from his earnest counsel.

Proverbs 27:9

Do not make friends with a hot-tempered man, do not associate with one easily angered, or you may learn his ways and get yourself ensnared.

Proverbs 22:24–25

Do not forsake your friend.

Proverbs 27:10

Jesus said, "You are my friends if you do what I command. I no longer call you servants, because a servant does not know his master's business. Instead, I have called you friends, for everything that I learned from my Father I have made known to you."

John 15:14–15

Jesus said, "My command is this: Love each other as I have loved you. Greater love has no one than this, that he lay down his life for his friends."

John 15:12–13

The LORD would speak to Moses face to face, as a man speaks with his friend.

Exodus 33:11

73

God's Words of Life on
FRIENDSHIP

Friendship with the world is hatred toward God. Anyone who chooses to be a friend of the world becomes an enemy of God.

James 4:4–5

He who loves a pure heart and whose speech is gracious will have the king for his friend.

Proverbs 22:11

A friend loves at all times.

Proverbs 17:17

Proverbs 17:17—How to Be a Good Friend
The Old Testament puts great emphasis on close family relationships. Surprisingly, Proverbs rates a good friend even higher, for he or she "sticks closer than a brother" (Proverbs 18:24). Fair-weather friends are common (Proverbs 14:20), and the wrong kind of companions will bring you trouble. But a true friend loves you at all times, even when things are bad.

Devotional Thought on
FRIENDSHIP

Some of my most cherished possessions are my school yearbooks. If my house ever caught fire, they'd be among the first things I'd grab as I ran outside. Penned in various colors of ink throughout the annuals are entries such as this:

"Your friendship means the world to me, and I'll never forget you or the times we shared. Love, Diana."

On adjacent pages are dozens of other entries, signed by other good friends: Helen, Sam, Donna, Jerry, Anita, Mark, Cyndee, and many others. Just seeing my friends' names is enough to flood my mind with endless memories.

Friendship was serious business with Christ. When his friends were hurting, he healed them. When they were hungry, he fed them. When they were discouraged, he prayed with them. And when they were dying, he cried for them.

Of course, it wasn't enough that he shed tears. He knew it would take blood. And so he said, "Greater love has no one than this, that one lay down his life for his friends." Shortly thereafter, at a place called Calvary, he put his life on the line for his friends.

The world hasn't gotten over it yet.

Blessed are those who mourn, for they will be comforted.

Matthew 5:4

On the Sabbath day Jesus went into the synagogue, as was his custom. The scroll of the prophet Isaiah was handed to him. Unrolling it, he found the place where it is written: "The Spirit of the Lord is on me, because he has anointed me to preach good news to the poor, to bind up the brokenhearted, to comfort all who mourn, and provide for those who grieve, to bestow on them a crown of beauty instead of ashes, the oil of gladness instead of mourning, and a garment of praise instead of a spirit of despair."

Luke 4:16-18 and Isaiah 61:1–3

The LORD is my shepherd, I shall not be in want. He makes me lie down in green pastures, he leads me beside quiet waters, he restores my soul. He guides me in paths of righteousness for his name's sake. Even though I walk through the valley of the shadow of death, I will fear no evil, for you are with me; your rod and your staff, they comfort me. You prepare a table before me in the presence of my enemies. You anoint my head with oil; my cup overflows. Surely goodness and love will follow me all the days of my life, and I will dwell in the house of the LORD forever.

Psalm 23

Listen, I tell you a mystery: We will not all sleep, but we will all be changed—in a flash, in the twinkling of an eye, at the last trumpet. For the trumpet will sound, the dead will be raised imperishable, and we will be changed. For the perishable must clothe itself with the imperishable, and the mortal with immortality. When the perishable has been clothed with the imperishable, and the mortal with immortality, then the saying that is written will come true: "Death has been swallowed up in victory. Where, O death, is your victory? Where, O death, is your sting?" The sting of death is sin, and the power of sin is the law. But thanks be to God! He gives us the victory through our Lord Jesus Christ.

1 Corinthians 15:51–57

Then I saw a new heaven and a new earth, for the first heaven and the first earth had passed away, and there was no longer any sea. I saw the Holy City, the new Jerusalem, coming down out of heaven from God, prepared as a bride beautifully dressed for her husband. And I heard a loud voice from the throne saying, "Now the dwelling of God is with men, and he will live with them. They will be his people, and God himself will be with them and be their God. He will wipe every tear from their eyes. There will be no more death or mourning or crying or pain, for the old order of things has passed away."

Revelation 21:1–4

"Lord," Martha said to Jesus, "if you had been here, my brother would not have died. But I know that even now God will give you whatever you ask." Jesus said to her, "Your brother will rise again." Martha answered, "I know he will rise again in the resurrection at the last day." Jesus said to her, "I am the resurrection and the life. He who believes in me will live, even though he dies; and whoever lives and believes in me will never die."

John 11:21–26

John 11:21—If Only …
Mary and Martha had very different personalities, but the same response to pain. Both sisters, meeting Jesus, said the same thing: "If you had been here, my brother would not have died" (John 11:21, 32). They had asked Jesus to come, and for reasons they could not understand, he had delayed. The healing they longed for had not occurred. Jesus gave the sisters no explanation of his timing, but showed he had a reason: to demonstrate his power over death.

GRIEF & DEATH

Jeff is the first true friend I've lost. It's difficult to describe what it feels like afterward. It's sort of like having an awesome view of the Pacific Ocean—the cliffs and sweeping sands of La Jolla, the distant peaks of Catalina Island, and in the foreground a favorite shade tree. And then a building is constructed that partially blocks the view. I can stand in that same spot and look out where I used to see the beautiful evergreen, always full of birds, and my spirit falls.

Maybe the tree is still there, but it is hidden behind an impenetrable barrier. All I know is that I can't see it anymore.

I can still see in the distance the breaking waves, the white sweeping sands, the gulls coasting on the wind, the faraway island peaks. But the tree, my favorite tree, is gone.

That's how it feels.

Some days I'd give anything to be able to talk with him again. But I know he's happy where he is and wouldn't want to be back. Where he is now, every tear has been wiped from his eyes, and there is no more death or crying or pain.

God's Words of Life on
GUIDANCE

The LORD will guide you always.

Isaiah 58:11

The LORD himself goes before you and will be with you; he will never leave you nor forsake you.

Deuteronomy 31:8

Delight yourself in the LORD and he will give you the desires of your heart. Commit your way to the LORD; trust in him and he will do this: He will make your righteousness shine like the dawn, the justice of your cause like the noonday sun.

Psalm 37:4-6

Trust in the LORD with all your heart and lean not on your own understanding; in all your ways acknowledge him, and he will make your paths straight.

Psalm 3:5–6

I will lead the blind by ways they have not known, along unfamiliar paths I will guide them; I will turn the darkness into light before them and make the rough places smooth, declares the LORD

Isaiah 42:16

God's Words of Life on
GUIDANCE

Jesus said, "I am the good shepherd; I know my sheep and my sheep know me. My sheep listen to my voice; I know them, and they follow me."

John 10:14, 27

Jesus said, "The Counselor, the Holy Spirit, whom the Father will send in my name, will teach you all things and will remind you of everything I have said to you."

John 14:26

When he, the Spirit of truth, comes, he will guide you into all truth.

John 16:13

The proverbs of Solomon son of David, king of Israel: for attaining wisdom and discipline; for understanding words of insight; for acquiring a disciplined and prudent life, doing what is right and just and fair; for giving prudence to the simple, knowledge and discretion to the young—let the wise listen and add to their learning, and let the discerning get guidance.

Proverbs 1:1–5

The law of the LORD is perfect, reviving the soul. The statutes of the LORD are trustworthy, making wise the simple. The precepts of the

God's Words of Life on
GUIDANCE

LORD are right, giving joy to the heart. The commands of the LORD are radiant, giving light to the eyes. The fear of the LORD is pure, enduring forever. The ordinances of the LORD are sure and altogether righteous. They are more precious than gold, than much pure gold; they are sweeter than honey, than honey from the comb.

Psalm 19:7–10

O, LORD, to all perfection I see a limit; but your commands are boundless. Oh, how I love your law! I meditate on it all day long.

Psalm 119:96–97

Psalm 119:96—Free At Last
People often wonder if following God's law will restrict them, but actual experience shows that God's law liberates—by freeing us from the destructive impact of sinful behavior, and by introducing us to the mind-expanding realm of God's wisdom. Like the author of Ecclesiastes, the psalmist had looked around and seen limits to everything. Only in following God's commands, he sees, can a person escape this frustrating sense of boundaries.

82

Devotional Thought on
GUIDANCE

Psalm 119 is a long, passionate love poem about God's law.

How do you fall in love with law? Most people admit that rules are necessary, and appreciate them grudgingly. But no one writes love poems to the federal drug abuse statutes.

The word translated "law" doesn't merely mean rules. It expresses the totality of God's written instructions. The poet sees life full of uncertainties, of enemies, of pain. But God has given a reliable guide for living—like pavement underfoot after you have been stuck in mud. Obeying God's law, to the psalmist, is no slavery—rather it is freedom. "I run in the path of your commands, for you have set my heart free" (Psalm 119:32).

God's laws channel God's love into the poet's life. They protect him from doing wrong and give him wisdom to understand his situation. They make new life flow into him. No wonder he writes with such thankfulness. In God's word he finds more than direction. He finds God himself.

God's Words of Life on
GUILT

Jesus said, "Come to me, all you who are weary and burdened, and I will give you rest."

Matthew 11:28

The teachers of the law and the Pharisees brought in a woman caught in adultery. They made her stand before the group and said to Jesus, "Teacher, this woman was caught in the act of adultery. In the Law Moses commanded us to stone such women. Now what do you say?" They were using this question as a trap, in order to have a basis for accusing him. But Jesus bent down and started to write on the ground with his finger. When they kept on questioning him, he straightened up and said to them, "If any one of you is without sin, let him be the first to throw a stone at her." Again he stooped down and wrote on the ground. At this, those who heard began to go away one at a time, the older ones first, until only Jesus was left, with the woman still standing there. Jesus straightened up and asked her, "Woman, where are they? Has no one condemned you?" "No one, sir," she said. "Then neither do I condemn you," Jesus declared.

John 8:3–11

The LORD is compassionate and gracious, slow to anger, abounding in love. He will not always accuse, nor will he harbor his anger forever; he does not treat us as our sins deserve or repay us according to our iniquities. For as high as the heavens are above the earth, so great is his love for those who fear him; as far as the east is from the west, so far has he removed our trans-gressions from us. As a father has compassion on his children, so the Lord has compassion on those who fear him.

Psalm 103:8–13

God is light; in him there is no darkness at all. If we claim to have fellowship with him yet walk in the darkness, we lie and do not live by the truth. But if we walk in the light, as he is in the light, we have fellowship with one another, and the blood of Jesus, his Son, purifies us from all sin. If we claim to be without sin, we deceive ourselves and the truth is not in us. If we confess our sins, he is faithful and just and will forgive us our sins and purify us from all unrighteousness.

1 *John* 1:5–9

Let us then approach the throne of grace with confidence, so that we may receive mercy and find grace to help us in our time of need.

Hebrews 4:16

When the woman saw that the fruit of the tree was good for food and pleasing to the eye, and

God's Words of Life on
GUILT

also desirable for gaining wisdom, she took some and ate it. She also gave some to her husband, who was with her, and he ate it. Then the eyes of both of them were opened, and they realized they were naked; so they sewed fig leaves together and made coverings for themselves. Then the man and his wife heard the sound of the LORD God as he was walking in the garden in the cool of the day, and they hid from the LORD God among the trees of the garden. But the LORD God called to the man, "Where are you?" He answered, "I heard you in the garden, and I was afraid because I was naked; so I hid."

Genesis 3:6–10

Genesis 3:7—Sin and Shame
When Adam and Eve disobeyed God, they immediately became ashamed of their bodies and wanted to hide. Ever since, sinful human beings have been "hiding" from each other and from God.

God asked Adam and Eve three questions, typical of the questions he puts to anyone "in hiding": 1) Where are you? (And why are you hiding from me?) 2) Who told you that you were naked? (And why did you believe somebody else, not me?) 3) What is this you have done? (And are you ready to take responsibility for it?)

Devotional Thought on
GUILT

People respond to guilt in different ways. Take Judas and Peter, for example. Both were trusted disciples, yet both turned on Christ. Judas betrayed him to a crowd of thugs and Hebrew zealots, leading to Christ's capture. And then when Christ was on trial for his life, Peter denied three times even knowing him. Both men were overwhelmed with guilt.

Judas wanted to advertise how sorry he felt, so he hung himself. On the other hand, Peter resolved his guilt before God and went on to become the key disciple in spreading the news of Christ.

Our reactions to guilt may not be as dramatic as were Judas's or Peter's. But our response can either drive us further from God or closer to him. The Bible makes it clear that God prefers the latter. He only asks that we admit our need and trust him with the load. And then we can walk in newness of life—precious, free, forgiven life.

God's Words of Life on
HONESTY

LORD, who may dwell in your sanctuary? Who may live on your holy hill? He whose walk is blameless and who does what is righteous, who speaks the truth from his heart and has no slander on his tongue, who does his neighbor no wrong and casts no slur on his fellowman, who despises a vile man but honors those who fear the LORD, who keeps his oath even when it hurts, who lends his money without usury and does not accept a bribe against the innocent. He who does these things will never be shaken.

Psalm 15

The LORD delights in men who are truthful.

Proverbs 12:22

The Lord says: "These people come near to me with their mouth and honor me with their lips, but their hearts are far from me."

Isaiah 29:13

Isaiah 29:13—Hypocrites
Again and again, Isaiah blasts the Israelites for a superficial faith—all words and no heart. Hundreds of years later, Jesus quoted this verse, saying that it applied precisely to people of his day (Mark 7:6–7).

Devotional Thought on
HONESTY

Lawrence is dishonest. Not in the sense that he says a lot of false things, but more in the sense that he acts differently around different people.

With his neighborhood buddies he curses like a sailor and drinks like a fish. With his church friends Lawrence talks about Jesus and acts like a model Christian.

Don't be swayed by the crowd. Stand up for the truth—all the time and everywhere you go! That's integrity—being complete or whole. It means being all that you are wherever you are. Acting one way here and another way there shows hypocrisy, not integrity.

Check your life for dishonest habits such as stealing, telling "little white lies," exaggerating, shading the truth, being two-faced, cheating, being fake, pretending to be nice, acting like things are okay when they aren't, bragging, or not practicing what you preach in some other way.

When you find an inconsistency, work with God on rooting it out of your life!

Suffering produces perseverance; perseverance, character; and character, hope. And hope
does not disappoint us, because God has
poured out his love into our hearts by the Holy
Spirit, whom he has given us.

Romans 5:3–5

Why are you downcast, O my soul? Why so dis-
turbed within me? Put your hope in God, for I
will yet praise him, my Savior and my God.

Psalm 42:11

May the God of hope fill you with all joy and
peace as you trust in him, so that you may
overflow with hope by the power of the Holy
Spirit.

Romans 15:13

I am the LORD; those who hope in me will not
be disappointed.

Isaiah 49:23

Praise be to the God and Father of our Lord
Jesus Christ! In his great mercy he has given us
new birth into a living hope through the resurrection of Jesus Christ from the dead, and into
an inheritance that can never perish, spoil or
fade—kept in heaven for you.

1 Peter 1:3–4

HOPE

No one whose hope is in you will ever be put to shame, but they will be put to shame who are treacherous without excuse. Show me your ways, O LORD, teach me your paths; guide me in your truth and teach me, for you are God my Savior, and my hope is in you all day long.

Psalm 25:3-5

We know that in all things God works for the good of those who love him, who have been called according to his purpose.

Romans 8:28

Though God slay me, yet will I hope in him.

Job 13:15

Even now my witness is in heaven; my advocate is on high. My intercessor is my friend as my eyes pour out tears to God; on behalf of a man he pleads with God as a man pleads for his friend.

Job 16:19–21

You have been my hope, O Sovereign LORD, my confidence since my youth.

Psalm 71:5

He gives strength to the weary and increases the power of the weak. Even youths grow tired and weary, and young men stumble and fall; but those who hope in the LORD will renew their strength. They will soar on wings like eagles; they will run and not grow weary, they will walk and not be faint.

Isaiah 40:29-31

I know that my Redeemer lives, and that in the end he will stand upon the earth. And after my skin has been destroyed, yet in my flesh I will see God.

Job 19:25–26

Job 19:25—An Outburst of Hope

In the midst of his deepest agony, Job expressed astonishing words of hope. This prophecy expands on two other flashes of hope (Job 9:33; 16:19–21). Job did not try to hide his despair and anguish, but, as this verse shows, the trials never crushed all of his hope.

Devotional Thought on
HOPE

All at once the world came crashing down on a single innocent man, a man named Job. It was the ultimate in unfairness.

First, raiders stole his belongings and slaughtered his servants. Then fire from the sky burned up his sheep, and a mighty wind destroyed his house and killed his sons and daughters. Finally, Job came down with a horrible, painful disease. *What did I do to deserve such suffering?*, he wailed.

Satan had claimed that people like Job love God only because of the good things he provides. Remove those good things, Satan challenged, and Job's faith would melt away along with his riches and health.

God's reputation was on the line. Would Job continue to trust him, even while his life was falling apart?

Like all grieving persons, Job went through emotional cycles. He whined, exploded, cajoled, and collapsed into self-pity. And occasionally he came up with a statement of brilliant hope.

Job's life stands as an example to every person who must go through great suffering.

God's Words of Life on
HUMILITY

Blessed are the meek, for they will inherit the earth.

Matthew 5:5

The disciples came to Jesus and asked, "Who is the greatest in the kingdom of heaven?" He called a little child and had him stand among them. And he said: "I tell you the truth, unless you change and become like little children, you will never enter the kingdom of heaven. Therefore, whoever humbles himself like this child is the greatest in the kingdom of heaven."

Matthew 18:1–4

God told Solomon, "If my people, who are called by my name, will humble themselves and pray and seek my face and turn from their wicked ways, then will I hear from heaven and will forgive their sin and will heal their land."

2 Chronicles 7:14

Moses was a very humble man, more humble than anyone else on the face of the earth.

Numbers 12:3

You, O LORD, save the humble but bring low those whose eyes are haughty.

Psalm 18:27

94

HUMILITY

He has showed you, O man, what is good.
And what does the LORD require of you? To act
justly and to love mercy and to walk humbly
with your God.

Micah 6:8

The LORD takes delight in his people; he
crowns the humble with salvation.

Psalm 149:4

With humility comes wisdom.

Proverbs 11:2

Humility and the fear of the LORD bring wealth
and honor and life.

Proverbs 22:4

Do not exalt yourself in the king's presence,
and do not claim a place among great men; it
is better for him to say to you, "Come up here,"
than for him to humiliate you before a noble-
man.

Proverbs 25:6–7

Do not be proud, but be willing to associate
with people of low position. Do not be
conceited.

Romans 12:16

God's Words of Life on
HUMILITY

All of you, clothe yourselves with humility toward one another, because, "God opposes the proud but gives grace to the humble." Humble yourselves, therefore, under God's mighty hand, that he may lift you up in due time.

1 Peter 5:5–6

Jesus replied, "If anyone wants to be first, he must be the very last, and the servant of all."

Mark 9:35

King David went in and sat before the LORD, and he said: "Who am I, O LORD God, and what is my family, that you have brought me this far?"

1 Chronicles 17:16

1 Chronicles 17:16—Rare Trait
King David possessed in abundance that rarest of qualities in a powerful ruler: humility. Ever mindful of his modest background, he credited God's grace, not his own merit, for his success.

Devotional Thought on

HUMILITY

Psalm 51 publishes David's anguished reaction when he was caught in sin. The story behind the psalm is told in 2 Samuel 11-12—a sordid tale of adultery, intrigue, and murder. David, the greatest king in Israel's history, acted like the worst.

David apparently thought nothing of his crime until the prophet Nathan accused him to his face. Then, in tears, David confessed.

All nations have heroes. Israel may have been alone in making heroic literature about its heroes' failings. In confessing his failures openly, David was certainly unique among all leaders of his day. He knew his place before God, and this humility made him an example for his people.

Ultimately Israel remembered David more for his devotion to God than for his military achievements. In centuries to come, Israel looked for a "son of David" to come and save them. They wanted a truly strong leader— one humble enough to know that God must lead the leaders.

God's Words of Life on
JOY

The fruit of the Spirit is ... joy.

Galatians 5:22

Rejoice in the Lord always. I will say it again:
Rejoice!

Philippians 4:4

This is the day the LORD has made; let us
rejoice and be glad in it.

Psalm 118:24

May the righteous be glad and rejoice before
God; may they be happy and joyful. Sing to
God, sing praise to his name, extol him who
rides on the clouds— his name is the LORD—
and rejoice before him.

Psalm 68:3–4

Shout aloud and sing for joy, for great is the
Holy One of Israel among you.

Isaiah 12:6

Though you have not seen him, you love him;
and even though you do not see him now, you
believe in him and are filled with an inexpress-
ible and glorious joy, for you are receiving the
goal of your faith, the salvation of your souls.

1 Peter 1:8–9

Is anyone happy? Let him sing songs of praise.

James 5:13

The angel said to them, "Do not be afraid. I bring you good news of great joy that will be for all the people. Today in the town of David a Savior has been born to you; he is Christ the Lord."

Luke 2:10–11

Say to those with fearful hearts, "Be strong, do not fear; your God will come." Then will the eyes of the blind be opened and the ears of the deaf unstopped. Then will the lame leap like a deer, and the mute tongue shout for joy.

Isaiah 35:4–6

The LORD your God is with you, he is mighty to save. He will take great delight in you, he will quiet you with his love, he will rejoice over you with singing.

Zephaniah 3:17

Consider it pure joy, my brothers, whenever you face trials of many kinds, because you know that the testing of your faith develops perseverance.

James 1:2–3

God's Words of Life on
JOY

The joy of the LORD is your strength.

Nehemiah 8:10

I Paul have learned to be content whatever the circumstances. I know what it is to be in need, and I know what it is to have plenty. I have learned the secret of being content in any and every situation, whether well fed or hungry, whether living in plenty or in want. I can do everything through Christ Jesus who gives me strength.

Philippians 4:11–13

Philippians 4:13—Paul's Secret
Shipwrecked, beaten, imprisoned, Paul had seen the down side of life. He had also known prosperity. Both, he suggests, offer temptations. But Paul had discovered a secret for contentment in all situations: his deeply personal sense of living in Christ. In this he found strength to handle anything.

Devotional Thought on
JOY

We think of joy as something you save up for months to experience and then splurge on in a moment of exhilaration: a trip to Disney World, a free-fall dive, a heart-stopping ride on the world's meanest roller coaster, a hot-air balloon trip. Paul had a different understanding of the word.

Philippians uses the word *joy* or *rejoice* every few paragraphs, but the joy it describes doesn't vanish after your heart starts beating normally again. Rejoice, says Paul, when someone selfishly tries to steal the limelight from you. And when you meet persecution for your faith. And when you are facing death.

In fact, the most joyous book in the Bible comes from the pen of an author chained to a Roman guard. Many scholars believe Paul wrote Philippians in Rome just about the time Nero began tossing Christians to ravenous lions. In such an environment, how could joy possibly thrive?

Paul summarized his life philosophy in a famous "to be or not to be" soliloquy, concluding that "to live is Christ and to die is gain" (Philippians 1:21). God is even stronger than death, and that makes a Christian's joy indestructible.

God's Words of Life on
KEEPING PROMISES

The fruit of the Spirit is … faithfulness.

Galatians 5:22

Moses said to the heads of the tribes of Israel: "This is what the LORD commands: When a man makes a vow to the LORD or takes an oath to obligate himself by a pledge, he must not break his word but must do everything he said."

Numbers 30:1–2

It is better not to vow than to make a vow and not fulfill it.

Ecclesiastes 5:5

Jonah replied to the Lord, "What I have vowed I will make good."

Jonah 2:9

He is the faithful God, keeping his covenant of love to a thousand generations of those who love him and keep his commands.

Deuteronomy 7:9

Jesus said, "You have heard that it was said to the people long ago, 'Do not break your oath, but keep the oaths you have made to the Lord.' But I tell you, Do not swear at all: either by heaven, for it is God's throne; or by the earth, for it is his footstool; or by Jerusalem, for it is the city of the Great King. And do not swear by your head, for you cannot make even one hair white or black. Simply let your 'Yes' be 'Yes,' and your 'No,' 'No'; anything beyond this comes from the evil one."

Matthew 5:33–37

The integrity of the upright guides them.

Proverbs 11:3

If you make a vow to the LORD your God, do not be slow to pay it, for the LORD your God will certainly demand it of you and you will be guilty of sin. Whatever your lips utter you must be sure to do, because you made your vow freely to the LORD your God with your own mouth.

Deuteronomy 23:21,23

The angel of the LORD called to Abraham from heaven and said, "I swear by myself, declares the LORD, that because you have done this and have not withheld your son, your only son, I will surely bless you and make your descendants as numerous as the stars in the sky and as the sand on the seashore. Your descendants will take possession of the cities of their enemies, and through your offspring all nations on earth will be blessed, because you have obeyed me."

Genesis 22:15–18

Genesis 22:18—Promises, Promises

When Abraham died, God's promises were far from fully realized. Abraham had only that one son to cling to. His only land was a burial plot. He still lived in a tent, and his only permanent structures were altars erected to worship the God who had made all those promises.

God, having promised him everything a man of that time could want, apparently wanted Abraham to think even bigger thoughts. He had slipped some words in along with the promises of offspring and land: "All peoples on earth will be blessed through you" (Genesis 12:3). God wanted to bless, not just Abraham, but the whole world.

Devotional Thought on
KEEPING PROMISES

W hen was the last time you heard anyone take full responsibility for a mistake they'd made? More often, we're pointing our finger in all directions, trying to find someone else to blame. And often our record isn't any better when it comes to telling the truth: many of us tend instead to say, true or not, whatever is most likely to get us the result we want.

We hate it when people break their promises to us. But are we any better at keeping our own promises?

There's an important standard of character that few people in our society are trying to follow. When you find someone who *is* following that standard—someone who tells the truth, keeps his or her promises, and takes responsibility for his or her behavior rather than trying to pass the blame on to someone else—latch onto that person! That's a person of integrity, someone whose life you can pattern your own after.

Keep your eyes open for people of integrity. We all need heroes, and it's hard to find a better definition of *hero* than this: a hero is someone who lives a life of integrity in a society that has forgotten what *integrity* means.

God's Words of Life on
LONELINESS

God has said, "Never will I leave you; never will I forsake you."

Hebrews 13:5

The Lord God said, "It is not good for the man to be alone. I will make a helper suitable for him."

Genesis 2:18

The widow who is really in need and left all alone puts her hope in God.

1 Timothy 5:5

Our fellowship is with the Father and with his Son, Jesus Christ.

1 John 1:3

May the grace of the Lord Jesus Christ, and the love of God, and the fellowship of the Holy Spirit be with you.

2 Corinthians 13:14

I am convinced that neither death nor life, neither angels nor demons, neither the present nor the future, nor any powers, neither height nor depth, nor anything else in all creation, will be able to separate us from the love of God that is in Christ Jesus our Lord.

Romans 8:38–39

I pray that you, being rooted and established in love, may have power, together with all the saints, to grasp how wide and long and high and deep is the love of Christ.

Ephesians 3:17–18

A father to the fatherless, a defender of widows, is God in his holy dwelling.

Psalm 68:5

Jesus often withdrew to lonely places and prayed.

Luke 5:16

Find rest, O my soul, in God alone; my hope comes from him. He alone is my rock and my salvation; he is my fortress, I will not be shaken.

Psalm 62:5-6

Jesus said, "Surely I am with you always."

Matthew 28:20

I call to God, and the LORD saves me.

Proverbs 55:16

God, who has called you into fellowship with his Son Jesus Christ our Lord is faithful.

1 Corinthians 1:9

Two disciples were going to a village called
Emmaus, about seven miles from Jerusalem.
They were talking with each other about everything that had happened. As they talked and
discussed these things with each other, Jesus
himself came up and walked along with them.

Luke 24:13–15

Luke 24:15—Final Glimpses of Jesus

Two of Jesus' disciples were walking away from
Jerusalem, downhearted. Their dream was
over; all the mounting hopes of the last few
years had died with Jesus on the cross.
A strange man appeared beside the two forlorn
disciples. Bizarrely, he seemed the only man
alive who hadn't heard about the incredible
week in Jerusalem. He talked with them, trac-
ing the whole story of the gospel, beginning
with Moses and the prophets.
The stranger intrigued them, and they asked
him to stay longer. At mealtime the last link
snapped into place. It was Jesus!

Devotional Thought on
LONELINESS

God's Word tells us that we are never alone. We may have feelings of loneliness, but the fact is that we always have a Friend in the Lord.

Writing about loneliness, Joyce Huggett notes the importance of understanding how much God loves you: "If you know yourself to be deeply loved by someone who will never let you down, fail you, or phase out of your life, you are rich in resources. This means that you do not spend your life searching for love. You have found it."

Have you found God's love? Have you embraced Christ?

Another good insight from Joyce Huggett: "Love is not dissipated when it is given away. It is replenished. If you want to find your way out of the maze of loneliness, therefore, you must give love."

What people in your life could use a little bit of your love today?

God's Words of Life on
LOVE

The fruit of the Spirit is love.

Galatians 5:22

This is how we know what love is: Jesus Christ laid down his life for us. And we ought to lay down our lives for our brothers. If anyone has material possessions and sees his brother in need but has no pity on him, how can the love of God be in him? Dear children, let us not love with words or tongue but with actions and in truth.

1 John 3:16–18

If I, Paul speak in the tongues of men and of angels, but have not love, I am only a resounding gong or a clanging cymbal. If I have the gift of prophecy and can fathom all mysteries and all knowledge, and if I have a faith that can move mountains, but have not love, I am nothing. If I give all I possess to the poor and surrender my body to the flames, but have not love, I gain nothing. Love is patient, love is kind. It does not envy, it does not boast, it is not proud. It is not rude, it is not self-seeking, it is not easily angered, it keeps no record of wrongs. Love does not delight in evil but rejoices with the truth. It always protects, always trusts, always hopes, always perseveres. Love never fails.

1 Corinthians 13:1–8

God's Words of Life on
LOVE

Dear friends, let us love one another, for love comes from God. Everyone who loves has been born of God and knows God. Whoever does not love does not know God, because God is love. This is how God showed his love among us: He sent his one and only Son into the world that we might live through him. This is love: not that we loved God, but that he loved us and sent his Son as an atoning sacrifice for our sins. Dear friends, since God so loved us, we also ought to love one another. No one has ever seen God; but if we love one another, God lives in us and his love is made complete in us.

1 John 4:7–12

And now these three remain: faith, hope and love. But the greatest of these is love.

1 Corinthians 13:13

We love because God first loved us.

1 John 4:19

If anyone says, "I love God," yet hates his brother, he is a liar. For anyone who does not love his brother, whom he has seen, cannot love God, whom he has not seen. And Jesus has given us this command: Whoever loves God must also love his brother.

1 John 4:20–21

God's Words of Life on
LOVE

Jesus said, "This is my command: Love each other."

John 15:17

Jesus said, "As I have loved you, so you must love one another. By this all men will know that you are my disciples, if you love one another."

John 13:34–35

What does the LORD your God ask of you but to fear the LORD your God, to walk in all his ways, to love him, to serve the LORD your God with all your heart and with all your soul?

Deuteronomy 10:12

Deuteronomy 10:12—More Than a Feeling
Twelve times Deuteronomy says we are to love God. In fact, Jesus was quoting Deuteronomy 6:5 when he gave the most important commandment as "Love the Lord your God with all your heart" (Mark 12:30). How can we love when we don't feel loving? In the Bible, love is more than a feeling. It is a decision to serve another person's interest. Only through God's help can this decision be made with "all your heart."

Devotional Thought on
LOVE

Love is not just another mark of a Christian, but the *birthmark* of a Christian.

When asked what the greatest commandment was, Christ replied, "Love the Lord your God with all your heart and with all your soul and with all your mind." The second, he said, was like it: "Love your neighbor as yourself." In other words, your life as a Christian should be marked first by your love for God, and then by your love for others and yourself.

Love for God. Your love for God can be measured by the amount of time you want to spend with him and by how much you allow him to influence your life. Is he a secret friend you're ashamed of, or is he someone you eagerly introduce others to?

Love for others. Love loves the unlovely, the unloving, the unlovable. It doesn't care if it's loved in return. Christian love turns a blind eye toward others' faults and keeps no record of wrong.

Love for yourself. Self-love is the recognition that you're a unique creation of God. He made *you* for a reason—with every scar and idiosyncrasy. You can love and accept yourself, because God first loved you!

God's Words of Life on
MONEY

No servant can serve two masters. Either he
will hate the one and love the other, or he will
be devoted to the one and despise the other.
You cannot serve both God and Money.

Luke 16:13

Now a man came up to Jesus and asked,
"Teacher, what good thing must I do to get
eternal life?" "Why do you ask me about what
is good?" Jesus replied. "There is only One who
is good. If you want to enter life, obey the
commandments." "Which ones?" the man
inquired. Jesus replied, "'Do not murder, do
not commit adultery, do not steal, do not give
false testimony, honor your father and mother,'
and 'love your neighbor as yourself.'" "All
these I have kept," the young man said. "What
do I still lack?" Jesus answered, "If you want to
be perfect, go, sell your possessions and give
to the poor, and you will have treasure in
heaven. Then come, follow me." When the
young man heard this, he went away sad,
because he had great wealth.

Matthew 19:16–22

Whatever was to my profit I Paul now consider
loss for the sake of Christ. What is more, I
consider everything a loss compared to the

surpassing greatness of knowing Christ Jesus my Lord, for whose sake I have lost all things. I consider them rubbish, that I may gain Christ.

Philippians 3:7–8

Jesus taught them saying, "Do not store up for yourselves treasures on earth, where moth and rust destroy, and where thieves break in and steal. But store up for yourselves treasures in heaven, where moth and rust do not destroy, and where thieves do not break in and steal. For where your treasure is, there your heart will be also."

Matthew 6:19–21

Command those who are rich in this present world not to be arrogant nor to put their hope in wealth, which is so uncertain, but to put their hope in God, who richly provides us with everything for our enjoyment. Command them to do good, to be rich in good deeds, and to be generous and willing to share. In this way they will lay up treasure for themselves as a firm foundation for the coming age, so that they may take hold of the life that is truly life.

1 Timothy 6:17–19

Keep your lives free from the love of money and be content with what you have.

Hebrews 13:5

God's Words of Life on
MONEY

Godliness with contentment is great gain. For we brought nothing into the world, and we can take nothing out of it. But if we have food and clothing, we will be content with that. People who want to get rich fall into temptation and a trap and into many foolish and harmful desires that plunge men into ruin and destruction. For the love of money is a root of all kinds of evil. Some people, eager for money, have wandered from the faith and pierced themselves with many griefs. But you, man of God, flee from all this, and pursue righteousness, godliness, faith, love, endurance and gentleness.

1 Timothy 6:6–11

Whoever sows sparingly will also reap sparingly, and whoever sows generously will also reap generously. Each man should give what he has decided in his heart to give, not reluctantly or under compulsion, for God loves a cheerful giver.

2 Corinthians 9:6–7

"Bring the whole tithe into the storehouse, that there may be food in my house. Test me in this," says the LORD Almighty, "and see if I will not throw open the floodgates of heaven and pour out so much blessing that you will not have room enough for it."

Malachi 3:10

Jesus said, "Give to the one who asks you, and do not turn away from the one who wants to borrow from you."

Matthew 5:42

While Jesus was in Bethany in the home of a man known as Simon the Leper, a woman came to him with an alabaster jar of very expensive perfume, which she poured on his head as he was reclining at the table. When the disciples saw this, they were indignant. "Why this waste?" they asked. "This perfume could have been sold at a high price and the money given to the poor." Aware of this, Jesus said to them, "Why are you bothering this woman? She has done a beautiful thing to me. The poor you will always have with you, but you will not always have me. When she poured this perfume on my body, she did it to prepare me for burial. I tell you the truth, wherever this gospel is preached throughout the world, what she has done will also be told, in memory of her."

Matthew 26:6–13

Jesus sat down opposite the place where the offerings were put and watched the crowd putting their money into the temple treasury. Many rich people threw in large amounts. But a poor widow came and put in two very small copper coins, worth only a fraction of a penny. Calling his disciples to him, Jesus said, "I tell you the truth, this poor widow has put more into the treasury than all the others. They all gave out of their wealth; but she, out of her poverty, put in everything—all she had to live on."

Mark 12:41–44

Someone in the crowd said to Jesus, "Teacher, tell my brother to divide the inheritance with me." Jesus replied, "Man, who appointed me a judge or an arbiter between you?" Then he said to them, "Watch out! Be on your guard against all kinds of greed; a man's life does not consist in the abundance of his possessions."

Luke 12:13–15

Luke 12:15—When Money Is Useless
Jesus refused to get involved in a family dispute about money. In this statement, he neatly summarized his usual approach to money. He did not condemn the possession of it. But he did warn against putting faith in money to secure the future. The rich man's money did him absolutely no good the night of his death. The lesson: Trust in God and his kingdom, and free yourself of worry about money and possessions.

Devotional Thought on
MONEY

The rich young ruler was a guy who seemed to have everything—youth, money, social status, power. He had even been faithful to God's Law since he was a kid. But he wanted assurance of eternal life, and he was devastated when Jesus told him to sell everything he had and give the money to the poor. Jesus knew that the young man was hanging on to his wealth and position as a security blanket. The rich young ruler loved his money more than he loved God.

People heavily involved in evangelism tell me that rich, comfortable people are often the hardest to reach with the gospel. Why? Because they feel they can take care of themselves; they don't think they need Jesus. And that often blinds them to other people's needs, too. Americans are better off financially than most people in the world. So American Christians have a special responsibility. Even though we're already saved, we need to check our hearts once in a while and make sure we're willing to spend a little less on ourselves and more on people who don't have as much as we do. We need to ask ourselves: *Do we love our money more than we love God?*

God's Words of Life on
MORALS & VALUES

God spoke all these words: "I am the LORD your God, you shall have no other gods before me. You shall not make for yourself an idol in the form of anything in heaven above or on the earth beneath or in the waters below. You shall not bow down to them or worship them; for I, the LORD your God, am a jealous God. You shall not misuse the name of the LORD your God, for the LORD will not hold anyone guiltless who misuses his name. Remember the Sabbath day by keeping it holy. Six days you shall labor and do all your work, but the seventh day is a Sabbath to the LORD your God. For in six days the LORD made the heavens and the earth, the sea, and all that is in them, but he rested on the seventh day. Therefore the LORD blessed the Sabbath day and made it holy. Honor your father and your mother, so that you may live long in the land the LORD your God is giving you. You shall not murder. You shall not commit adultery. You shall not steal. You shall not give false testimony against your neighbor. You shall not covet your neighbor's house. You shall not covet your neighbor's wife, or his manservant or maidservant, his ox or donkey, or anything that belongs to your neighbor."

Exodus 20:1–5,7-17

This is the covenant I will make with them after that time, says the Lord. I will put my laws in their hearts, and I will write them on their minds.

Hebrews 10:16

All Scripture is God-breathed and is useful for teaching, rebuking, correcting and training in righteousness, so that the man of God may be thoroughly equipped for every good work.

2 Timothy 3:16–17

My son, keep your father's commands and do not forsake your mother's teaching. Bind them upon your heart forever; fasten them around your neck. When you walk, they will guide you; when you sleep, they will watch over you; when you awake, they will speak to you. For these commands are a lamp, this teaching is a light, and the corrections of discipline are the way to life.

Proverbs 6:20–23

Do not be carried away by all kinds of strange teachings.

Hebrews 13:9

See to it that no one takes you captive through hollow and deceptive philosophy, which

121

depends on human tradition and the basic
principles of this world rather than on Christ.

Colossians 2:8

We demolish arguments and every pretension
that sets itself up against the knowledge of
God, and we take captive every thought to
make it obedient to Christ.

2 Corinthians 10:5

Do not conform any longer to the pattern of
this world, but be transformed by the renewing
of your mind.

Romans 12:2

Hate what is evil; cling to what is good.

Romans 12:9

Romans 12:9—Down-to-Earth Problems

Too often theology is viewed as stuff for her-
mits and marooned shipwreck victims. When
there's nothing else to do, then is the time to
ask abstract questions about God. Such a
notion would surely have exasperated the
apostle Paul. To him, theology was worthless
unless it made a difference in how people
lived. Paul did not live as an intellectual
recluse. He applied his theology to life,
practicing what he preached.

MORALS & VALUES

As a young man, Daniel could have antici-pated an outstanding future in Jerusalem. He came from a prominent family, and he had a first-rate mind (Daniel 1:4). But, when the Babylonian army dragged him captive to a faraway country, they didn't ask about his plans and dreams.

Through his ability and God's blessing he rose to the post of prime minister of Babylon. Yet he remained an outsider. The higher he rose, the more prominent a target he became. Babylonians resented his foreign background and his political success. Their plots put him under pressure to compromise his faith, to fit in, to bend his principles. His life was often at risk.

Daniel's career near the top lasted at least 66 years, so that by the time he was thrown into the lions' den (Daniel 6), he must have been in his 80s. Throughout these years, he labored with great effectiveness for Babylon. He was respectful and diligent, even though working for pagan kings. Yet he never compro-mised his faith. He would not bend, even when threatened with death. The Bible gives no bet-ter model of how to live with and serve those who don't share or respect your beliefs.

God's Words of Life on
OBEDIENCE

What good is it, my brothers, if a man claims to have faith but has no deeds? Can such faith save him? Suppose a brother or sister is without clothes and daily food. If one of you says to him, "Go, I wish you well; keep warm and well fed," but does nothing about his physical needs, what good is it? In the same way, faith by itself, if it is not accompanied by action, is dead. The scripture was fulfilled that says, "Abraham believed God, and it was credited to him as righteousness," and he was called God's friend. You see that a person is justified by what he does and not by faith alone. As the body without the spirit is dead, so faith without deeds is dead.

James 2:14–17, 23–24, 26

This is what the LORD Almighty, the God of Israel, says: "Obey me, and I will be your God and you will be my people. Walk in all the ways I command you, that it may go well with you."

Jeremiah 7:21, 23

Blessed are they whose ways are blameless, who walk according to the law of the LORD. Blessed are they who keep his statutes and seek him with all their heart. They do nothing wrong; they walk in his ways.

Psalm 119:1–3

Jesus taught them saying, "Love the Lord your God with all your heart and with all your soul and with all your mind. This is the first and greatest commandment. And the second is like it: Love your neighbor as yourself." All the Law and the Prophets hang on these two commandments."

Matthew 22:37–40

We know that we have come to know him if we obey his commands. The man who says, "I know him," but does not do what he commands is a liar, and the truth is not in him. But if anyone obeys his word, God's love is truly made complete in him.

1 John 2:3–5

Jesus said, "If you love me, you will obey what I command."

John 14:15

What does the LORD your God ask of you but to fear the LORD your God, to walk in all his ways, to love him, to serve the LORD your God with all your heart and with all your soul, and to observe the LORD's commands and decrees?

Deuteronomy 10:12–13

God's Words of Life on
OBEDIENCE

Jesus said, "Not everyone who says to me, 'Lord, Lord,' will enter the kingdom of heaven, but only he who does the will of my Father who is in heaven."

Matthew 7:21

To obey is better than sacrifice.

1 Samuel 15:22

Do not merely listen to the word, and so deceive yourselves. Do what it says.

James 1:22

The secret things belong to the LORD our God, but the things revealed belong to us and to our children forever, that we may follow all the words of this law.

Deuteronomy 29:29

Deuteronomy 29:29—God's Secrets
"I don't understand why God is doing this," people say. But God hasn't told us everything. Our finite minds could not possibly grasp some things, and other information is simply unnecessary or unhelpful for us to know. What God has told us (in his law, for instance) he intends for us to obey.

OBEDIENCE

Deuteronomy repeats verbatim many of the laws given in Exodus, Leviticus, and Numbers. Yet it is far from a rulebook. A different spirit pervades it: the spirit of love. The rules in Deuteronomy read more like a guide on "How to Have a Successful Family" than, say, an automobile maintenance manual. To keep up a car you need only follow the rules. To maintain a close personal relationship you need more—you need love.

Deuteronomy focuses on motives: *why* people should obey laws. The preceding three books barely mentioned the love of God for his people, but Deuteronomy again and again refers to it (see Deuteronomy 4:37; 7:7–8; 10:15; 23:5). The author portrays God as a father with his children, as a mother who gives them life, as an eagle hovering over its young.

In return, God asks for obedience based on love, not on a sense of duty. At least 15 times in the book Moses tells the Israelites to love God and cling to him. God wants not just an outward conformity, but an obedience that comes from the heart.

God's Words of Life on
PATIENCE

As God's chosen people, holy and dearly loved, clothe yourselves with compassion, kindness, humility, gentleness and patience.

Colossians 3:12

The fruit of the Spirit is … patience.

Galatians 5:22

The Lord is patient with you, not wanting anyone to perish, but everyone to come to repentance.

2 Peter 3:9

Be patient, then, brothers, until the Lord's coming. See how the farmer waits for the land to yield its valuable crop and how patient he is for the autumn and spring rains. You too, be patient and stand firm, because the Lord's coming is near.

James 5:7–8

A patient man has great understanding, but a quick-tempered man displays folly.

Proverbs 14:29

A man's wisdom gives him patience; it is to his glory to overlook an offense.

Proverbs 19:11

After waiting patiently, Abraham received what was promised.

Hebrews 6:15

Love is patient.

1 Corinthians 13:4

Be completely humble and gentle; be patient, bearing with one another in love. Make every effort to keep the unity of the Spirit through the bond of peace.

Ephesians 4:2–3

And we urge you, brothers, warn those who are idle, encourage the timid, help the weak, be patient with everyone. Make sure that nobody pays back wrong for wrong, but always try to be kind to each other and to everyone else.

1 Thessalonians 5:14-15

Be still before the LORD and wait patiently for him.

Psalm 37:7

The end of the matter is better than its beginning, and patience is better than pride.

Ecclesiastes 7:8

You, O Lord, will keep in perfect peace him whose mind is steadfast, because he trusts in you.

Isaiah 26:3

Create in me a pure heart, O God, and renew a steadfast spirit within me.

Psalm 51:10

King David said, "I have stilled and quieted my soul; like a weaned child with its mother, like a weaned child is my soul within me. O Israel, put your hope in the LORD both now and forevermore."

Psalm 131:2–3

Psalm 131:2—A Child with Its Mother

How trusting is a baby? Not very, some would say, for babies cry violently as soon as they feel the slightest hunger. It is the weaned child, a little older, who has learned to trust its mother, to fret less and simply ask for food instead of wailing. The profound simplicity of this patience is David's model for how he, and all Israel, should wait on the Lord.

Devotional Thought on
PATIENCE

Perhaps you've seen those lapel buttons that read: "PBPGINFWMY." *Please be patient—God is not finished with me yet.* You are God's special project—he is at work in your life, but he's not done.

Just as God hasn't given up on you, so you shouldn't give up on others who also are God's workmanship. Each person (Christian or not) is of infinite value to the Lord—created in God's image—and in each, his "construction project" is at a different stage of completion. Knowing how patient God has been with you should help you demonstrate patience toward others and enable you to "bear with one another in love," as Paul writes.

God works patiently. He doesn't spot something negative in your life and then twist your arm or beat you with a stick until you make it right. He loves you until you, of your own free will, decide you want what he wants. God's patience toward you is not unique—it's how he responds to everyone because patience is part of his character. And he wants it to be part of yours, too.

God's Words of Life on
PEACE

Jesus said, "Peace I leave with you; my peace I give you. I do not give to you as the world gives. Do not let your hearts be troubled and do not be afraid."

John 14:27

Do not be anxious about anything, but in everything, by prayer and petition, with thanksgiving, present your requests to God. And the peace of God, which transcends all understanding, will guard your hearts and your minds in Christ Jesus.

Philippians 4:6–7

Christ himself is our peace.

Ephesians 2:14

The fear of the LORD leads to life: Then one rests content, untouched by trouble.

Proverbs 19:23

Jesus said, "Take my yoke upon you and learn from me, for I am gentle and humble in heart, and you will find rest for your souls."

Matthew 11:29

I will lie down and sleep in peace, for you alone, O LORD, make me dwell in safety.

Psalm 4:8

The LORD gives strength to his people; the LORD blesses his people with peace.

Psalm 29:11

Great peace have they who love your law, and nothing can make them stumble.

Psalm 119:165

May the God of hope fill you with all joy and peace as you trust in him.

Romans 15:13

Turn from evil and do good; seek peace and pursue it.

Psalm 34:14

A heart of peace gives life to the body, but envy rots the bones.

Proverbs 14:30

When a man's ways are pleasing to the LORD, he makes his enemies live at peace with him.

Proverbs 16:7

LORD, you establish peace for us; all that we have accomplished you have done for us.

Isaiah 26:12

PEACE

How beautiful on the mountains are the feet of those who bring good news, who proclaim peace, who bring good tidings, who proclaim salvation, who say to Zion, "Your God reigns!"

Isaiah 52:7

Though the mountains be shaken and the hills be removed, yet my unfailing love for you will not be shaken nor my covenant of peace be removed," says the LORD, who has compassion on you.

Isaiah 54:10

Those who walk uprightly enter into peace; they find rest as they lie in death.

Isaiah 57:2

"I have told you these things, so that in me you may have peace. In this world you will have trouble. But take heart! I have overcome the world."

John 16:33

Let the peace of Christ rule in your hearts, since as members of one body you were called to peace. And be thankful.

Colossians 3:15

God's Words of Life on
PEACE

Since we have been justified through faith, we have peace with God through our Lord Jesus Christ, through whom we have gained access by faith into this grace in which we now stand. And we rejoice in the hope of the glory of God.

Romans 5:1–2

The mind controlled by the Spirit is life and peace.

Romans 8:6

Make every effort to do what leads to peace and to mutual edification.

Romans 14:19

God has called us to live in peace.

1 Corinthians 7:15

For God is not a God of disorder but of peace.

1 Corinthians 14:33

Make every effort to keep the unity of the Spirit through the bond of peace.

Ephesians 4:3

May the Lord of peace himself give you peace at all times and in every way. The Lord be with you.

2 Thessalonians 3:16

God's Words of Life on
PEACE

Flee the evil desires of youth, and pursue righteousness, faith, love and peace, along with those who call on the Lord out of a pure heart.

2 Timothy 2:22

Mercy, peace and love be yours in abundance.

Jude 1:2

The fruit of the Spirit is peace.

Galatians 5:22

O LORD, you will keep in perfect peace him whose mind is steadfast, because he trusts in you.

Isaiah 26:3

Isaiah 26:3—Perfect Peace
Isaiah, who lived in a time of tremendous turmoil, predicted more of the same. Godly people would suffer along with everybody else, he said. How should believers cope? Isaiah urged them to focus on a reality greater than their current troubles: to keep their minds steady on God, who never loses control over events.

We sense it at rare moments. The first real day of spring, when the air is heavy with the scent of blooms and new life sprouts everywhere. Or even in winter, when an unexpected snowstorm clothes a gray, dingy city in pure white. Or when we watch a baby animal at play in the zoo. Or remember the first sudden twinge of romantic love.

This world may be full of pollution, war, crime, and hate. But inside us, all of us, linger remnants that remind us of what the world could be like—of what *we* could be like. The Old Testament prophets dreamed of "that day" when creation would be made new. And those sensations burst out of the last few chapters of Revelation. That perfect world is not merely a dream; it will come true.

There will be no more tears then, nor pain. Wild animals will frolic, not kill. Once again creation will work the way God intended. Peace will reign not only between God and individuals, but between him and all creation.

God's Words of Life on
PERSEVERANCE

We also rejoice in our sufferings, because we know that suffering produces perseverance; perseverance, character; and character, hope. And hope does not disappoint us, because God has poured out his love into our hearts by the Holy Spirit, whom he has given us.

Romans 5:3-5

Thanks be to God! He gives us the victory through our Lord Jesus Christ. Therefore, my dear brothers, stand firm. Let nothing move you. Always give yourselves fully to the work of the Lord, because you know that your labor in the Lord is not in vain.

1 Corinthians 15:57–58

Watch out that you do not lose what you have worked for, but that you may be rewarded fully. Anyone who runs ahead and does not continue in the teaching of Christ does not have God; whoever continues in the teaching has both the Father and the Son.

2 John 1:8–9

Blessed is the man who perseveres under trial, because when he has stood the test, he will receive the crown of life that God has promised to those who love him.

James 1:12

PERSEVERANCE

Do you not know? Have you not heard? The LORD is the everlasting God, the Creator of the ends of the earth. He will not grow tired or weary, and his understanding no one can fathom. He gives strength to the weary and increases the power of the weak. Even youths grow tired and weary, and young men stumble and fall; but those who hope in the LORD will renew their strength. They will soar on wings like eagles; they will run and not grow weary, they will walk and not be faint.

Isaiah 40:28–31

Everyone who competes in the games goes into strict training. They do it to get a crown that will not last; but we do it to get a crown that will last forever. Therefore I do not run like a man running aimlessly; I do not fight like a man beating the air. No, I beat my body and make it my slave so that after I have preached to others, I myself will not be disqualified for the prize.

1 Corinthians 9:25–27

Pursue righteousness, godliness, faith, love, endurance and gentleness. Fight the good fight of the faith.

1 Timothy 6:11–12

God's Words of Life on
PERSEVERANCE

Since we are surrounded by such a great cloud of witnesses, let us throw off everything that hinders and the sin that so easily entangles, and let us run with perseverance the race marked out for us.

Hebrews 12:1

Hebrews 12:1—Pep Talk
The early Christians who first read this book were facing persecution, and their faith was bending under the pressure. Think of the "great cloud of witnesses" who have gone before, Hebrews urges, and fix your eyes on Jesus, who volunteered to die on your behalf. With its imagery borrowed from athletics, this portion of Hebrews sounds like a coach's half-time speech delivered to competitors in danger of giving up.

PERSEVERANCE

One of the most successful movies of all time was the original *Rocky*—the roaches-to-riches story of an untested Philadelphia brawler who was given a chance to box the world champion.

Rocky didn't doubt it would be a tough fight—he simply wanted to complete the 15 grueling rounds, to remain standing at the final bell. In his words, he wanted to "go the distance."

In a fight of another sort the apostle Paul faced similar staggering odds. His was a spiritual battle, yet he maintained the same goal of "going the distance." If you think Rocky had it tough, read 2 Corinthians 11:24–33. It's Paul's account of the beatings, whippings, stonings, shipwrecks, imprisonments, and threats he faced in his "fight of the faith." Yet he endured and persevered through every trial, temptation, discouragement and despair.

In the "fight of the faith," the odds sometimes seem staggering. You face temptations daily that blitz your belief. You face moral decisions that others never have to consider. Yet the Bible indicates an eternal prize awaits those who remain faithful to the final bell.

God's Words of Life on
PRAYER

My soul thirsts for God, for the living God.

Psalm 42:2

Pray in the Spirit on all occasions with all kinds of prayers and requests.

Ephesians 6:18

Jesus often withdrew to lonely places and prayed.

Luke 5:16

We do not know what we ought to pray for, but the Spirit himself intercedes for us with groans that words cannot express.

Romans 8:26

The prayer of a righteous man is powerful and effective. Elijah was a man just like us. He prayed earnestly that it would not rain, and it did not rain on the land for three and a half years. Again he prayed, and the heavens gave rain, and the earth produced its crops.

James 5:16–18

Jesus said, "Everything is possible for him who believes."

Mark 9:23

Jesus replied, "I tell you the truth, if you have faith and do not doubt, you can say to this mountain, 'Go, throw yourself into the sea,' and it will be done. If you believe, you will receive whatever you ask for in prayer."

Matthew 21:18–22

This is the confidence we have in approaching God: that if we ask anything according to his will, he hears us. And if we know that he hears us—whatever we ask—we know that we have what we asked of him.

1 *John* 5:14–15

Ah, Sovereign LORD, you have made the heavens and the earth by your great power and outstretched arm Nothing is too hard for you.

Jeremiah 32:17

Jesus replied, "I will do whatever you ask in my name, so that the Son may bring glory to the Father. You may ask me for anything in my name, and I will do it."

John 14:13–14

Jesus replied, "Ask and you will receive, and your joy will be complete."

John 16:24

God's Words of Life on
PRAYER

Delight yourself in the LORD and he will give you the desires of your heart.

Psalm 37:4

God answered their prayers, because they trusted in him.

1 Chronicles 5:20

They devoted themselves to the apostles' teaching and to the fellowship, to the breaking of bread and to prayer.

Acts 2:42

Be joyful always; pray continually; give thanks in all circumstances, for this is God's will for you in Christ Jesus.

1 Thessalonians 5:16-18

The king said to me, "What is it you want?" Then I prayed to the God of heaven, and I answered the king.

Nehemiah 2:4–5

Nehemiah 2:4—The "Arrow Prayer"
Nehemiah characteristically prayed to God while he went about his duties. He even "shot an arrow" to God, silently asking him for help in the middle of this crucial conversation with the king. He spontaneously inserted prayers as he wrote his memoirs.

Devotional Thought on
PRAYER

You would be deeply hurt if someone you loved never spoke to you unless he wanted something. God does want you to ask him for the things you need—but prayer is much more than that. It's a conversation between two people who love each other. In this case, one of those people is God. But it won't be much of a conversation if you don't *talk* to him about the things that are important to you, about your hopes and dreams and fears and disappointments. He wants to hear your expressions of love for him and your thanks for the many things he has given you. Don't wait until you need something to talk to God.

Be aware of God's presence; talk to him all day long. In the morning, silently thank him for the sunrise. Before you read your devotions, ask him to show you what he wants for the day. On the way to school, ask him to help you remember what you have studied for that important test. If you could see Jesus by your side all day, you would talk to him constantly. Well, he's really there—and he would like to talk with you.

God's Words of Life on
PRIDE

This is what the LORD says: "Let not the wise man boast of his wisdom or the strong man boast of his strength or the rich man boast of his riches, but let him who boasts boast about this: that he understands and knows me, that I am the LORD, who exercises kindness, justice and righteousness on earth."

Jeremiah 9:23–24

The LORD detests all the proud of heart.

Proverbs 16:5

Now listen, you who say, "Today or tomorrow we will go to this or that city, spend a year there, carry on business and make money." Why, you do not even know what will happen tomorrow. What is your life? You are a mist that appears for a little while and then vanishes. Instead, you ought to say, "If it is the Lord's will, we will live and do this or that." As it is, you boast and brag. All such boasting is evil.

James 4:13–16

Pride goes before destruction, a haughty spirit before a fall.

Proverbs 16:18

God opposes the proud but gives grace to the humble.

James 4:6

The LORD Almighty has a day in store for all the proud and lofty, for all that is exalted (and they will be humbled). The arrogance of man will be brought low and the pride of men humbled; the LORD alone will be exalted in that day.

Isaiah 2:12, 17

A man's pride brings him low, but a man of lowly spirit gains honor.

Proverbs 29:23

Brothers, think of what you were when you were called. Not many of you were wise by human standards; not many were influential; not many were of noble birth. But God chose the foolish things of the world to shame the wise; God chose the weak things of the world to shame the strong. He chose the lowly things of this world and the despised things—and the things that are not—to nullify the things that are, so that no one may boast before him. It is because of him that you are in Christ Jesus, who has become for us wisdom from God—that is, our righteousness, holiness and redemption. Therefore, as it is written: "Let him who boasts boast in the Lord."

1 Corinthians 1:26–31

God's Words of Life on
PRIDE

Let us not become conceited, provoking and envying each other.

Galatians 5:26

Do not think of yourself more highly than you ought, but rather think of yourself with sober judgment, in accordance with the measure of faith God has given you.

Romans 12:3

The king will show no regard for the gods of his fathers or for the one desired by women, nor will he regard any god, but will exalt himself above them all.

Daniel 11:37

Daniel 11:37—Exalted above the Gods
The tyrant Antiochus IV, whom most commentators believe is described here, minted many coins showing his portrait. The early coins were merely stamped, "King Antiochus." But, as he grew more obsessed with his own importance, he added features to his portrait that made him look like the Greek gods Apollo or Zeus, and to his given name he appended the title "Epiphanes"—"God Manifest." Such behavior earned him the nickname "Antiochus Epimanes"—"crazy Antiochus."

Devotional Thought on
PRIDE

When I knew Susan, she had everything going for her: good grades, good looks, good job. Then she was in a car accident and was never the same.

"Now I know," she once told me, "how it feels to be on the other side of the fence, to feel like you're a nobody because you don't look like the girls in *Glamour*.

"All my life," she said, "I was programmed to think success. I had it all. And I couldn't understand why other people weren't as together as me, you know? It was like I was the yardstick, and they didn't measure up. And God may have been somewhere out there, but I didn't need him because I was doing fine on my own.

"But now I understand—that I didn't understand anything before. The needs and hurts of others? Didn't see them. Never noticed because I was all that mattered.

"Now? I'm not so full of myself," she continued. "And when there's less of me, there's more room for God."

God's Words of Life on
REPENTANCE

King David said to Nathan, "I have sinned against the LORD." Nathan replied, "The LORD has taken away your sin."

2 Samuel 12:13

Jesus told them this parable: "Suppose one of you has a hundred sheep and loses one of them. Does he not leave the ninety-nine in the open country and go after the lost sheep until he finds it? And when he finds it, he joyfully puts it on his shoulders and goes home. Then he calls his friends and neighbors together and says, 'Rejoice with me; I have found my lost sheep.' I tell you that in the same way there will be more rejoicing in heaven over one sinner who repents than over ninety-nine righteous persons who do not need to repent."

Luke 15:3–7

Jesus continued: "There was a man who had two sons. The younger one said to his father, 'Father, give me my share of the estate.' So he divided his property between them. Not long after that, the younger son got together all he had, set off for a distant country and there squandered his wealth in wild living. After he had spent everything, he began to be in need. So he went and hired himself out to a citizen of that country, who sent him to his fields to feed pigs. He longed to fill his stomach with the pods that the pigs were eating, but no one gave him anything. When he came to his senses, he said, 'How many of my father's hired men have food to spare, and here I am starving to death! I will set out and go back to my father and say to him: Father, I have sinned against heaven and against you. I am no longer worthy to be called your son; make me like one of your hired men.' So he got up and went to his father. But while he was still a long way off, his father saw him and was filled with compassion for him; he ran to his son, threw his arms around him and kissed him. The son said to him, 'Father, I have sinned against heaven and against you. I am no longer worthy to be called your son.' But the father said to his servants, 'Quick! Bring the best robe and put it on him. Put a ring on his finger and sandals on his feet. Bring the fattened calf and kill it. Let's have a feast and celebrate. For this son of mine was dead and is alive again; he was lost and is found.'"

Luke 15:11–24

Repent and be baptized, every one of you, in the name of Jesus Christ for the forgiveness of your sins. And you will receive the gift of the Holy Spirit. The promise is for you and your

children and for all who are far off—for all
whom the Lord our God will call.

Acts 2:38

Repent then, and turn to God, so that your sins
may be wiped out, that times of refreshing may
come from the Lord.

Acts 3:19

While Ezra was praying and confessing, weeping
and throwing himself down before the house of
God, a large crowd of Israelites—men, women
and children—gathered around him. They too
wept bitterly.

Ezra 10:1

Ezra 10:1—Unprecedented Response

Israelites were marrying their idolatrous neighbors. At the news, Ezra completely lost his com-
posure, tore his clothes, and sat down stunned
(Ezra 9:3). His grief-filled prayer of repentance
inspired a large crowd to join him in bitter
weeping. Then and there they resolved to break
up the marriages. Ezra's grief over Israel's spiritual compromise was similar to that of many
prophets. But the people's response to Ezra was
unprecedented. Pre-exile prophets like Amos or
Jeremiah never saw such heartfelt repentance.
Evidently the exile really had purified Israel.

Devotional Thought on
REPENTANCE

Picture it another scene, Nehemiah 8: a vast, hushed crowd watching as Ezra ascends a newly built platform in the square. As he opens the book, they stand up. They praise God, hands lifted high; then they bow down, faces in the dirt. Ezra begins to read. His helpers circulate in the crowd, explaining and interpreting what God's Word says. The people listen attentively. And then a strange sound begins to rise, spreading through the multitude. It is the sound of weeping.

The Law Ezra read was very ancient, but that day marked something new. The Jews were becoming, in a way they had never been before, a people of the book. They were being rebuilt, with material as strong as the stones in their newly built city wall.

A single man atop a wooden platform, reading from a simple scroll. Yet the words he reads, carefully explained to all, show their power in the way they affect those who hear them. The people are moved to praise God, to weep over their sins, to change their behavior, and to make renewed promises to God.

God's Words of Life on
RESPONSIBILITY

Jesus taught them saying, "You are the light of the world. A city on a hill cannot be hidden. Neither do people light a lamp and put it under a bowl. Instead they put it on its stand, and it gives light to everyone in the house. In the same way, let your light shine before men, that they may see your good deeds and praise your Father in heaven."

Matthew 5:13–16

Each of you should look not only to your own interests, but also to the interests of others.

Philippians 2:4

Jesus replied, "From everyone who has been given much, much will be demanded; and from the one who has been entrusted with much, much more will be asked."

Luke 12:48

The man who had received the five talents brought the other five. "Master," he said, "you entrusted me with five talents. See, I have gained five more." His master replied, "Well done, good and faithful servant! You have been faithful with a few things; I will put you in charge of many things. Come and share your master's happiness!"

Matthew 25:20–21

Jesus replied, "Whoever can be trusted with very little can also be trusted with much."

Luke 16:10

God reconciled us to himself through Christ and gave us the ministry of reconciliation.

2 Corinthians 5:18

Jesus came to his disciples and said, "All authority in heaven and on earth has been given to me. Therefore go and make disciples of all nations, baptizing them in the name of the Father and of the Son and of the Holy Spirit, and teaching them to obey everything I have commanded you."

Matthew 28:18–20

Fear God and keep his commandments, for this is the whole duty of man.

Ecclesiastes 12:13

Acknowledge the God of your father, and serve him with wholehearted devotion and with a willing mind, for the LORD searches every heart and understands every motive behind the thoughts. If you seek him, he will be found by you.

1 Chronicles 28:9

God's Words of Life on
RESPONSIBILITY

Today I have made you a fortified city, an iron pillar and a bronze wall to stand against the whole land—against the kings of Judah, its officials, its priests and the people of the land.

Jeremiah 1:18

Jeremiah 1:18—*Too Young?*
Like Moses before him, Jeremiah responded reluctantly to God's call. "I am only a child," he protested, feeling too inexperienced to carry such responsibility (Jeremiah 1:6). But God contradicted him. Age and experience did not matter; God's presence did (Jeremiah 1:8). In the face of powerful opposition, God would make Jeremiah as strong as iron.

RESPONSIBILITY

It is one thing to represent the governor of your state; it is quite another to represent God and use his name. Yet Jesus had exactly that plan in mind for his followers. He hand-selected simple folk like James and Andrew to bear his name and represent him to the world. In the same way that a governor or president delegates authority to people acting on his behalf, Jesus gave his followers his own authority and power.

Jesus' time on earth was running out. Luke 9:51 records that he "resolutely set out for Jerusalem," on his way to die. Only a few weeks remained for him to train those people who would be left behind to carry his name: "Christ-ians." Jesus used the time as a crash training course for his followers.

Later, the apostle Paul would say that we, the church, actually form Christ's body in the world. By coming to earth and then leaving, Jesus ushered in a completely new chapter in history. And, as he prepared for departure, he called on his people—the disciples and us—to represent him. In every sense, we bear his name.

God's Words of Life on
SEEKING GOD'S WILL

The Counselor, the Holy Spirit, whom the Father will send in my name, will teach you all things and will remind you of everything I have said to you.

John 14:26

We have not stopped praying for you and asking God to fill you with the knowledge of his will through all spiritual wisdom and understanding. And we pray this in order that you may live a life worthy of the Lord and may please him in every way: bearing fruit in every good work, growing in the knowledge of God.

Colossians 1:9–10

Blessed is the man who does not walk in the counsel of the wicked or stand in the way of sinners or sit in the seat of mockers. But his delight is in the law of the LORD, and on his law he meditates day and night. He is like a tree planted by streams of water, which yields its fruit in season and whose leaf does not wither. Whatever he does prospers.

Psalm 1:1–3

Be joyful always; pray continually; give thanks in all circumstances, for this is God's will for you.

1 Thessalonians 5:16–18

SEEKING GOD'S WILL

All Scripture is God-breathed and is useful for teaching, rebuking, correcting and training in righteousness, so that the man of God may be thoroughly equipped for every good work.

2 Timothy 3:16–17

The world and its desires pass away, but the man who does the will of God lives forever.

1 John 2:17

Those who live according to the sinful nature have their minds set on what that nature desires; but those who live in accordance with the Spirit have their minds set on what the Spirit desires.

Romans 8:5

May the God of peace, who through the blood of the eternal covenant brought back from the dead our Lord Jesus, that great Shepherd of the sheep, equip you with everything good for doing his will, and may he work in us what is pleasing to him, through Jesus Christ, to whom be glory for ever and ever. Amen.

Hebrews 13:20–21

Jesus prayed, "Father, not my will, but yours be done."

Luke 22:42

God's Words of Life on
SEEKING GOD'S WILL

It is God who works in you to will and to act according to his good purpose.

Philippians 2:13

Gideon said to God, "If you will save Israel by my hand as you have promised—look, I will place a wool fleece on the threshing floor. If there is dew only on the fleece and all the ground is dry, then I will know that you will save Israel by my hand, as you said." And that is what happened. Gideon rose early the next day; he squeezed the fleece and wrung out the dew—a bowlful of water.

Judges 6:36–38

Judges 6:37—Putting Out a Fleece

How much proof of God's will does one person need? Though the angel of the Lord had assured Gideon of success, he took fright and wanted to double-check, then triple-check, by asking for miracles. In some circles today, "putting out a fleece" has come to mean asking God to do something unusual to confirm his guidance. However, Gideon's action seems more like a lack of faith than a model of seeking God's guidance.

Devotional Thought on
SEEKING GOD'S WILL

Until you and I know what God's will is for us, how do we decide about things like marriage? And jobs? What classes should you take next semester? What about relationships? Where should you go to college?

We can know God's will. Paul tells us how in Romans 12:1-2:

"Therefore, I urge you, brothers, in view of God's mercy, to offer your bodies as living sacrifices, holy and pleasing to God—this is your spiritual act of worship. Do not conform any longer to the pattern of this world, but be transformed by the renewing of your mind. Then you will be able to test and approve what God's will is—his good, pleasing and perfect will."

In those two verses, Paul lays it out almost like a formula. I can know God's will for my life if I: (1) Give God my body as a living sacrifice, (2) Give God my will by letting him control my life, and (3) Give God my mind by keeping it pure and flooding it with his Word.

Do those three things, Paul says and we can prove what God's will is—his good, pleasing, and perfect will.

SELF-ESTEEM

You, O LORD, created my inmost being; you knit me together in my mother's womb. I praise you because I am fearfully and wonderfully made; your works are wonderful, I know that full well.

Psalm 139:13–14

O LORD, when I consider your heavens, the work of your fingers, the moon and the stars, which you have set in place, what is man that you are mindful of him, the son of man that you care for him? You made him a little lower than the heavenly beings and crowned him with glory and honor. You made him ruler over the works of your hands; you put everything under his feet: all flocks and herds, and the beasts of the field, the birds of the air, and the fish of the sea, all that swim the paths of the seas.

Psalm 8:3–8

The LORD appeared to us in the past, saying: "I have loved you with an everlasting love; I have drawn you with loving-kindness."

Jeremiah 31:3

Jesus said, "Are not five sparrows sold for two pennies? Yet not one of them is forgotten by God. Indeed, the very hairs of your head are all numbered. Don't be afraid; you are worth more than many sparrows."

Luke 12:6–7

SELF–ESTEEM

The word of the LORD came to me, saying, "Before I formed you in the womb I knew you, before you were born I set you apart; I appointed you as a prophet to the nations." "Ah, Sovereign LORD," I said, "I do not know how to speak; I am only a child." But the LORD said to me, "Do not say, 'I am only a child.' You must go to everyone I send you to and say whatever I command you."

Jeremiah 1:4–7

Don't let anyone look down on you because you are young, but set an example in speech, in life, in love, in faith and in purity.

1 Timothy 4:12

This is what the LORD says—he who created you, he who formed you, "I have redeemed you; I have summoned you by name; you are mine. You are precious and honored in my sight, and I love you."

Isaiah 43:1, 4

The LORD God formed the man from the dust of the ground and breathed into his nostrils the breath of life, and the man became a living being.

Genesis 2:7

In love God predestined us to be adopted as his sons through Jesus Christ.

Ephesians 1:4–5

God's Words of Life on
SELF-ESTEEM

For God so loved the world that he gave his one and only Son, that whoever believes in him shall not perish but have eternal life.

John 3:16

It was not with perishable things such as silver or gold that you were redeemed but with the precious blood of Christ.

1 Peter 1:18–19

We are God's workmanship, created in Christ Jesus to do good works, which God prepared in advance for us to do.

Ephesians 2:10

God created man in his own image, in the image of God he created him; male and female he created them.

Genesis 1:27

Genesis 2:7—Where We Came From

Genesis 1–3 pays humanity its highest compliment. After making all the glories of the world, God topped off his work with man and woman. He put them in charge. Unlike the animals, they were like him, "in his image." "Very good," he said to himself when he had finished. With humans he quit, satisfied.

Devotional Thought on
SELF–ESTEEM

Y ou were valuable enough to God that he
was willing to give the life of his only
Son. As the dad of two children, I can tell
you this: That price is higher than I would be
willing to pay. I don't know your name or
anything about you, yet I believe I would be
willing to risk my life to save yours. But I
could never give the lives of either of my
children to save yours. I wouldn't do it even
if you could convince me you deserved it.

God did for you what I could not bring
myself to do. God loved you so much that he
freely *gave his only Son* so that you might have
eternal life. That's how much he valued your
life. The Creator of the universe paid the
highest price that can be paid to give you
the chance to experience a personal relationship with God through Jesus Christ, to
be totally forgiven of your sins, and to live
forever. *You are priceless*. He knows both the
bad and the good about you, and he still
loves you.

God's Words of Life on
SEXUAL PURITY

Blessed are the pure in heart, for they will see God.

Matthew 5:8

Flee from sexual immorality. All other sins a man commits are outside his body, but he who sins sexually sins against his own body. Do you not know that your body is a temple of the Holy Spirit, who is in you, whom you have received from God? You are not your own; you were bought at a price. Therefore honor God with your body.

1 Corinthians 6:18–20

Do not offer the parts of your body to sin, as instruments of wickedness, but rather offer your-selves to God, as those who have been brought from death to life; and offer the parts of your body to him as instruments of righteousness.

Romans 6:13

The body is not meant for sexual immorality, but for the Lord.

1 Corinthians 6:13

Whatever is true, whatever is noble, whatever is right, whatever is pure, whatever is lovely, what-ever is admirable—if anything is excellent or praiseworthy—think about such things.

Philippians 4:8

God's Words of Life on

SEXUAL PURITY

It is God's will that you should be sanctified: that you should avoid sexual immorality; that each of you should learn to control his own body in a way that is holy and honorable. God did not call us to be impure, but to live a holy life.

1 Thessalonians 4:3–4, 7

Offer your bodies as living sacrifices, holy and pleasing to God—this is your spiritual act of worship.

Romans 12:1

Everything in the world—the cravings of sinful man, the lust of his eyes and the boasting of what he has and does—comes not from the Father but from the world. The world and its desires pass away, but the man who does the will of God lives forever.

1 John 2:16–17

Jesus taught them saying, "You have heard that it was said, 'Do not commit adultery.' But I tell you that anyone who looks at a woman lustfully has already committed adultery with her in his heart."

Matthew 5:27–28

I made a covenant with my eyes not to look lustfully at a girl.

Job 31:1

God's Words of Life on
SEXUAL PURITY

How can a young man keep his way pure? By living according to your word, O LORD.

Psalm 119:9

Take captive every thought to make it obedient to Christ.

2 Corinthians 10:5

Create in me a pure heart, O God, and renew a steadfast spirit within me.

Psalm 51:10

Set your minds on things above, not on earthly things. For you died, and your life is now hidden with Christ in God.

Colossians 3:2–3

Do not arouse or awaken love until it so desires.

Song of Songs 3:5

Song of Songs 3:5—Let Love Sleep

If love is so wonderful, as this poem beautifully sings, shouldn't people pursue it recklessly? Yet the beloved warns them not to. Three times she urges others not to force love, but to let it develop at its own rate. Love should wait for its proper time.

Devotional Thought on
SEXUAL PURITY

As Jesus put it, "Whatever God has joined together, let man not separate" (Matthew 19:6). If you're not ready to commit yourself for a lifetime of loving, don't get "joined" in sexual intercourse.

The Bible says that when you go to bed, something happens to the two of you, something that changes you at the deepest level. You are bound together body and soul. You can't just painlessly back away from the relationship any more than you can separate two pieces of paper that have been glued together. You can tear the two pieces apart, but not without leaving pieces of one stuck forever to the other. Paul talks about that in 1 Corinthians 6:12–20.

Sex is an incredible gift in the right context. In the wrong context it's an incredible source of heartbreak and lifebreak. You don't want to join two lives together unless you are as sure as is humanly possible they will never be torn apart again. That means marriage—full-hearted, committed marriage.

Don't kid yourself into thinking that *feelings*, however strong, are a substitute.

God's Words of Life on
SPIRITUAL GIFTS

Each man has his own gift from God.

1 Corinthians 7:7

There are different kinds of gifts, but the same Spirit. There are different kinds of service, but the same Lord. There are different kinds of working, but the same God works all of them in all men. Now to each one the manifestation of the Spirit is given for the common good. To one there is given through the Spirit the message of wisdom, to another the message of knowledge by means of the same Spirit, to another faith by the same Spirit, to another gifts of healing by that one Spirit, to another miraculous powers, to another prophecy, to another distinguishing between spirits, to another speaking in different kinds of tongues, and to still another the interpretation of tongues. All these are the work of one and the same Spirit, and he gives them to each one, just as he determines.

1 Corinthians 12:4–11

Just as each of us has one body with many members, and these members do not all have the same function, so in Christ we who are many form one body, and each member belongs to all the others. We have different gifts, according to the grace given us. If a man's gift is prophesying, let him use it in proportion to his faith. If it is serving, let him serve; if it is teaching, let him teach; if it is encouraging, let him encourage; if it is contributing to the needs of others, let him give generously; if it is leadership, let him govern diligently; if it is showing mercy, let him do it cheerfully.

Romans 12:4–8

The body is a unit, though it is made up of many parts; and though all its parts are many, they form one body. So it is with Christ. For we were all baptized by one Spirit into one body— whether Jews or Greeks, slave or free—and we were all given the one Spirit to drink. Now the body is not made up of one part but of many. If the foot should say, "Because I am not a hand, I do not belong to the body," it would not for that reason cease to be part of the body. And if the ear should say, "Because I am not an eye, I do not belong to the body," it would not for that reason cease to be part of the body. If the whole body were an eye, where would the sense of hearing be? If the whole body were an ear, where would the sense of smell be? But in fact God has arranged the parts in the body of

God's Words of Life on
SPIRITUAL GIFTS

Christ, every one of them, just as he wanted them to be.

1 Corinthians 12:12–18

Each one should use whatever gift he has received to serve others, faithfully administering God's grace in its various forms. If anyone speaks, he should do it as one speaking the very words of God. If anyone serves, he should do it with the strength God provides, so that in all things God may be praised through Jesus Christ.

1 Peter 4:10–11

To one the Master gave five talents of money, to another two talents, and to another one talent, each according to his ability.

Matthew 25:15

Matthew 25:15–30—Original Talent

Today when we speak of a "talented" musician or athlete, we are actually harking back to this parable. A talent in Jesus' time was a valuable sum of money worth about two years' wages. Because of this parable, the word acquired a different meaning. Each person in the kingdom of heaven is given a certain number of gifts and opportunities ("talents") to serve God. We can either waste those opportunities or invest them in a way that furthers the kingdom.

Devotional Thought on
SPIRITUAL GIFTS

Can you get along in life without eyes? Of course, but you must make adjustments. You must rely more on other senses and depend on friends, or perhaps a seeing-eye dog, for extra help. Regardless of what adjustments you make, however, your body will remain incomplete without eyes. You will miss out on color and design and all the visual delights this world offers.

An eyeless body can cope, but a bodyless eye is unimaginable. The most beautiful eyes in the world, when detached from a body, are lifeless and worthless. Eyes need a body that will bring them blood and receive their nerve impulses.

In 1 Corinthians 12, Paul gives a clever anatomy lesson, with a purpose. By comparing members of the church of Christ to parts of a human body, he neatly explains two complementary truths. Any part of a body, he says— such as an eye or a foot—makes a valuable contribution to the whole body. Whenever a single member is missing, the entire body suffers.

And, he continues, no member can survive if isolated from the rest. Alone, an eye is useless. All parts must cooperate to form a single, unified body.

God's Words of Life on
SPIRITUAL GROWTH

Jesus replied, "Blessed are those who hunger and thirst for righteousness, for they will be filled."

Matthew 5:6

He has showed you, O man, what is good. And what does the LORD require of you? To act justly and to love mercy and to walk humbly with your God.

Micah 6:8

This is what the LORD says: "Let him who boasts boast about this: that he understands and knows me, that I am the Lord, who exercises kindness, justice and righteousness on earth, for in these I delight."

Jeremiah 9:23–24.

Jesus said, "I am the vine; you are the branches. If a man remains in me and I in him, he will bear much fruit; apart from me you can do nothing. If anyone does not remain in me, he is like a branch that is thrown away and withers; such branches are picked up, thrown into the fire and burned. If you remain in me and my words remain in you, ask whatever you wish, and it will be given you. This is to my Father's glory, that you bear much fruit, showing yourselves to be my disciples.

John 15:5–8

SPIRITUAL GROWTH

Be on your guard so that you may not be carried away by the error of lawless men and fall from your secure position. But grow in the grace and knowledge of our Lord and Savior Jesus Christ.

2 Peter 3:17–18

Let us leave the elementary teachings about Christ and go on to maturity.

Hebrews 6:1

When I, Paul, was a child, I talked like a child, I thought like a child, I reasoned like a child. When I became a man, I put childish ways behind me.

1 Corinthians 13:11

God's divine power has given us everything we need for life and godliness through our knowledge of him who called us by his own glory and goodness. Through these he has given us his very great and precious promises, so that through them you may participate in the divine nature and escape the corruption in the world caused by evil desires. For this very reason, make every effort to add to your faith goodness; and to goodness, knowledge; and to knowledge, self-control; and to self-control, perseverance; and to perseverance, godliness;

and to godliness, brotherly kindness; and to
brotherly kindness, love. For if you possess
these qualities in increasing measure, they will
keep you from being ineffective and unproduc-
tive in your knowledge of our Lord Jesus
Christ.

2 Peter 1:3–8

May God himself, the God of peace, sanctify
you through and through.

1 Thessalonians 5:23

Paul wrote, pray also that the eyes of your
heart may be enlightened in order that you
may know the hope to which God has called
you, the riches of his glorious inheritance in
the saints, and his incomparably great power
for us who believe.

Ephesians 1:18–19

"You will seek me and find me when you seek
me with all your heart. I will be found by you,"
declares the LORD.

Jeremiah 29:13–14

Paul wrote, I want to know Christ and the
power of his resurrection and the fellowship of
sharing in his sufferings, becoming like him in

his death, and so, somehow, to attain to the resurrection from the dead. Not that I have already obtained all this, or have already been made perfect, but I press on to take hold of that for which Christ Jesus took hold of me. Brothers, I do not consider myself yet to have taken hold of it. But one thing I do: Forgetting what is behind and straining toward what is ahead, I press on toward the goal to win the prize for which God has called me heavenward in Christ Jesus.

Philippians 3:10–14

Paul wrote, we have not stopped praying for you and asking God to fill you with the knowledge of his will through all spiritual wisdom and understanding. And we pray this in order that you may live a life worthy of the Lord and may please him in every way: bearing fruit in every good work, growing in the knowledge of God, being strengthened with all power according to his glorious might so that you may have great endurance and patience, and joyfully giving thanks to the Father, who has qualified you to share in the inheritance of the saints in the kingdom of light.

Colossians 1:9–12

God's Words of Life on
SPIRITUAL GROWTH

Train yourself to be godly. For physical training is of some value, but godliness has value for all things, holding promise for both the present life and the life to come.

1 Timothy 4:7–8

1 Timothy 4:7–8—Athlete in Training

Paul uses the analogy of physical training in his letter to Timothy, urging him to train himself for godliness the same way disciplined athletes train for competition. Athletes must overcome physical barriers; Timothy faced personality barriers. Several times Paul refers to Timothy's reserved, timid disposition.
Given his shyness and his half-Jewish, half-Gentile ancestry, Timothy did not seem the ideal choice for a heresy fighter in a turbulent church. But Paul was convinced he could do the job.

SPIRITUAL GROWTH

Picture God as a master jeweler and yourself as a priceless diamond in the rough. Paul probably had something like that in mind when he wrote, "We are God's workmanship." Each of us is of infinite value to the Lord. And he is at work, shaping, cutting, filing, grinding, buffing, and polishing until every facet of our lives reflects his artistry.

God is a gentle craftsman. He doesn't pound away with a cold chisel and sledge hammer. He works delicately and slowly, with small, precise strokes, through the convincing power of his Spirit.

We are his workmanship, but as yet we're uncompleted projects. So be patient. We can't expect to be perfect and always act the right way or say the right things. We may lose our temper when provoked, talk behind someone's back, or covet another's looks, abilities, or success. God doesn't ignore these things—it's just that cutting and shaping take time. Philippians 1:6 says we can be confident "that the God who started this great work in you would keep at it and bring it to a flourishing finish on the very day Christ Jesus appears."

STRESS

The Israelites looked up, and there were the Egyptians, marching after them. They were terrified and cried out to the Lord. They said to Moses, "Was it because there were no graves in Egypt that you brought us to the desert to die? What have you done to us by bringing us out of Egypt? Didn't we say to you in Egypt, 'Leave us alone; let us serve the Egyptians'? It would have been better for us to serve the Egyptians than to die in the desert!" Moses answered the people, "Do not be afraid. Stand firm and you will see the deliverance the Lord will bring you today. The Lord will fight for you; you need only to be still."

Exodus 14:10–14

For God, who said, "Let light shine out of darkness, made his light shine in our hearts to give us the light of the knowledge of the glory of God in the face of Christ. But we have this treasure in jars of clay to show that this all-supassing power is from God and not from us. We are hard pressed on every side, but not crushed; perplexed, but not in despair; persecuted, but not abandoned; struck down, but not destroyed."

2 Corinthians 4:6–9

O LORD, you are my God; I will exalt you and praise your name. You have been a refuge for the poor, a refuge for the needy in his distress, a shelter from the storm and a shade from the heat.

Isaiah 25:1, 4

The LORD is my rock, my fortress and my deliverer; my God is my rock, in whom I take refuge. He is my shield and the horn of my salvation, my stronghold.

Psalm 18:2

Surely God is my salvation; I will trust and not be afraid. The LORD, the LORD, is my strength and my song; he has become my salvation.

Isaiah 12:2

The LORD is good, a refuge in times of trouble. He cares for those who trust in him.

Nahum 1:7

The LORD said to Joshua, "Do not be afraid; do not be discouraged."

Joshua 8:1

Be still, and know that I am God.

Psalm 46:10

God's Words of Life on
STRESS

Jesus replied, "When you hear of wars and rumors of wars, do not be alarmed. Such things must happen, but the end is still to come."

Mark 13:7

Assyria will fall by a sword that is not of man.

Isaiah 31:8

Isaiah 31:8—A Time of Crisis

Hezekiah, cowering under siege in Jerusalem, turned to Isaiah for advice. Should he surrender? Assyrian soldiers were already pressing in around the walls, hurling insults at the demoralized citizens inside. Isaiah recommended prayer and reliance on the power of God. Have faith, he said; don't surrender, don't fear. Assyria will return home, wounded (Isaiah 37:5–7). Isaiah's deep courage and optimism raised the morale of all Jerusalem. And in a spectacular way (Isaiah 37:36; also 2 Kings 19), God took care of the Assyrian army.

Devotional Thought on
STRESS

From one day to the next, one year to the next, newspaper headlines and CNN broadcasts don't seem to change. Armies invade neighboring countries. Assassins topple governments. Earthquakes level major cities. Politicians steal the public blind. Something else causes cancer.

If you're anything like me, you sometimes feel overwhelmed by the chaos of life and people around you. There are days when nothing or no one makes sense, and you're convinced you're the last surviving sane person. On days when I feel like that, it helps me to tell God and get the burden off my shoulders. That doesn't mean things will change overnight, or necessarily at all. It just makes me feel better to know God understands how I feel.

In James 4:8 the Bible says, "Come near to God and he will come near to you." *The Message* puts it this way: "Say a quiet *yes* to God and he'll be there in no time." So take God up on the promise by talking to him on those days you feel as helpless as a wind-tossed rag. It's great relief to sense God's presence. He wants to be the still point of your turning, twisting, ever-changing world.

God's Words of Life on
SUBSTANCE ABUSE

Do not get drunk on wine, which leads to debauchery. Instead, be filled with the Spirit.

Ephesians 5:18

Woe to those who rise early in the morning to run after their drinks, who stay up late at night till they are inflamed with wine. They have harps and lyres at their banquets, tambourines and flutes and wine, but they have no regard for the deeds of the LORD, no respect for the work of his hands.

Isaiah 5:11–12

Don't you know that you yourselves are God's temple and that God's Spirit lives in you? If anyone destroys God's temple, God will destroy him; for God's temple is sacred, and you are that temple.

1 Corinthians 3:16–17

The hour has come for you to wake up from your slumber, because our salvation is nearer now than when we first believed. The night is nearly over; the day is almost here. So let us put aside the deeds of darkness and put on the armor of light. Let us behave decently, as in the daytime, not in orgies and drunkenness, not in sexual immorality and debauchery, not in dissension and jealousy. Rather, clothe yourselves with the Lord Jesus Christ, and do not think about how to gratify the desires of the sinful nature.

Romans 13:11–14

Wine is a mocker and beer a brawler; whoever is led astray by them is not wise.

Proverbs 20:1

He who loves pleasure will become poor; whoever loves wine and oil will never be rich.

Proverbs 21:17

Do not join those who drink too much wine or gorge themselves on meat, for drunkards and gluttons become poor, and drowsiness clothes them in rags.

Proverbs 23:20–21

For we know that our old self was crucified with Jesus so that the body of sin might be done away with, that we should no longer be slaves to sin—because anyone who has died has been freed from sin.

Romans 6:6–7

Do not let sin reign in your mortal body so that you obey its evil desires. Do not offer the parts of your body to sin, as instruments of wickedness, but rather offer yourselves to God, as those who have been brought from death to life; and offer the parts of your body to him as instruments of righteousness. For sin shall not be your master, because you are not under law, but under grace.

Romans 6:12–14

Who has woe? Who has sorrow? Who has strife? Who has complaints? Who has needless bruises? Who has bloodshot eyes? Those who linger over wine, who go to sample bowls of mixed wine. Do not gaze at wine when it is red, when it sparkles in the cup, when it goes down smoothly! In the end it bites like a snake and poisons like a viper. Your eyes will see strange sights and your mind imagine confusing things. You will be like one sleeping on the high seas, lying on top of the rigging. "They hit me," you will say, "but I'm not hurt! They beat me, but I don't feel it! When will I wake up so I can find another drink?"

Proverbs 23:29–35

Proverbs 23:35—The Dangers of Wine

Wine was common in biblical times, but its dangers were recognized. Proverbs contains some of the Bible's strongest warnings against overindulgence.

Devotional Thought on

SUBSTANCE ABUSE

For two nightmarish years at Devlin High, Sheila was heavily involved with cocaine.

She's now drug-free. It wasn't easy—three months of isolation in a rehabilitation hospital followed by lots of counseling—but Sheila has come face to face with one of life's greatest mysteries.

"With not much else to do in the hospital, I started reading the Bible my mom sent me. And it hit me—like never before—that drugs are a big lie. They can't bring happiness or take away your pain. Only Jesus can do that."

We can never find real satisfaction or long-term happiness in drugs (or any other selfish pursuit). True fulfillment is found only in Christ.

The "Just Say No!" campaign is only a partial answer to the drug problem. People who say no to drugs—if they don't know Christ—still have emotional needs. Granted, they may not turn to drugs, but they will continue to look for something to fill the holes in their souls.

A more complete answer to the drug problem? "Just Say No! (to drugs)—Just Say Yes! (to Christ)."

My comfort in my suffering is this: Your promise preserves my life, O LORD.

Psalm 119:50

Jesus said, "In this world you will have trouble. But take heart! I have overcome the world."

John 16:33

There was given me a thorn in my flesh, a messenger of Satan, to torment me. Three times I pleaded with the Lord to take it away from me. But he said to me, "My grace is sufficient for you, for my power is made perfect in weakness." Therefore I will boast all the more gladly about my weaknesses, so that Christ's power may rest on me. That is why, for Christ's sake, I delight in weaknesses, in insults, in hardships, in persecutions, in difficulties. For when I am weak, then I am strong.

2 Corinthians 12:7–10

Consider it pure joy, my brothers, whenever you face trials of many kinds, because you know that the testing of your faith develops perseverance. Perseverance must finish its work so that you may be mature and complete, not lacking anything. Blessed is the man who perseveres under trial, because when he has stood the test, he will receive the crown of life that God has promised to those who love him.

James 1:2–4, 12

The God of all grace, who called you to his eternal glory in Christ, after you have suffered a little while, will himself restore you and make you strong, firm and steadfast.

1 Peter 5:10

For a little while you may have had to suffer grief in all kinds of trials. These have come so that your faith—of greater worth than gold, which perishes even though refined by fire—may be proved genuine and may result in praise, glory and honor when Jesus Christ is revealed.

1 Peter 1:6–7

Do not be surprised at the painful trial you are suffering, as though something strange were happening to you. But rejoice that you participate in the sufferings of Christ, so that you may be overjoyed when his glory is revealed. If you are insulted because of the name of Christ, you are blessed, for the Spirit of glory and of God rests on you. If you suffer, it should not be as a murderer or thief or any other kind of criminal, or even as a meddler. However, if you suffer as a

God's Words of Life on
SUFFERING

Christian, do not be ashamed, but praise God that you bear that name. Those who suffer according to God's will should commit themselves to their faithful Creator and continue to do good.

1 Peter 4:12–16, 19

Our light and momentary troubles are achieving for us an eternal glory that far outweighs them all.

2 Corinthians 4:17

When God has tested me, I will come forth as gold.

Job 23:10

Those who suffer God delivers in their suffering; he speaks to them in their affliction.

Job 36:15

Job 36:15—What Job Teaches about Suffering

Job affirms that God is not deaf to our cries and is in control of this world no matter how it looks. God did not answer all Job's questions, but his very appearance caused Job's doubts to melt away. Job learned that God cared about him and that God rules the world.

Devotional Thought on
SUFFERING

Do Christians have car accidents? Do they get cancer? Are they ever fired from their jobs? The answer to all three questions is, of course, yes. But that answer causes big problems for some new Christians. Doesn't the Bible promise that God will look out for and protect his followers?

People puzzled by such questions often refer to Old Testament books where God clearly promised success and protection to the Israelites.

God asked only one thing in return: follow the covenant agreement

God predicted bluntly, "When I have brought them into the land flowing with milk and honey and when they eat their fill and thrive, they will turn to other gods and worship them, rejecting me and breaking my covenant" (Deuteronomy 31:20).

Deuteronomy may offer a clue to why God does not exempt his followers from every bad thing in life. Ironically, prosperity and health may make it harder to depend on God. The Israelites proved least faithful to God after they moved into the prosperity of the promised land. In the desert, at least, they had been forced to lean on God just for daily survival. But after a very short time in Canaan, they forgot about him.

God's Words of Life on
TEMPTATION

No temptation has seized you except what is common to man. And God is faithful; he will not let you be tempted beyond what you can bear. But when you are tempted, he will also provide a way out so that you can stand up under it.

1 Corinthians 10:13

When tempted, no one should say, "God is tempting me." For God cannot be tempted by evil, nor does he tempt anyone.

James 1:13

Jesus was led by the Spirit into the desert to be tempted by the devil. After fasting forty days and forty nights, he was hungry. The tempter came to him and said, "If you are the Son of God, tell these stones to become bread." Jesus answered, "It is written: 'Man does not live on bread alone, but on every word that comes from the mouth of God.'" Then the devil took him to the holy city and had him stand on the highest point of the temple. "If you are the Son of God," he said, "throw yourself down. For it is written: 'He will command his angels concerning you, and they will lift you up in their hands, so that you will not strike your foot against a stone.'" Jesus answered him, "It is also written: 'Do not

put the Lord your God to the test.'" Again, the
devil took him to a very high mountain and
showed him all the kingdoms of the world and
their splendor. "All this I will give you," he said,
"if you will bow down and worship me." Jesus
said to him, "Away from me, Satan! For it is
written: 'Worship the Lord your God, and serve
him only.'" Then the devil left him, and angels
came and attended him.

Matthew 4:1–11

Resist the devil, and he will flee from you.

James 4:7

Let us hold firmly to the faith we profess. For
we do not have a high priest who is unable to
sympathize with our weaknesses, but we have
one who has been tempted in every way, just
as we are—yet was without sin. Let us then
approach the throne of grace with confidence,
so that we may receive mercy and find grace to
help us in our time of need.

Hebrews 4:14–16

Be strong in the Lord and in his mighty power.
Put on the full armor of God so that you can
take your stand against the devil's schemes.
For our struggle is not against flesh and blood,

but against the rulers, against the authorities, against the powers of this dark world and against the spiritual forces of evil in the heavenly realms. Therefore put on the full armor of God, so that when the day of evil comes, you may be able to stand your ground, and after you have done everything, to stand. Stand firm then, with the belt of truth buckled around your waist, with the breastplate of righteousness in place, and with your feet fitted with the readiness that comes from the gospel of peace. In addition to all this, take up the shield of faith, with which you can extinguish all the flaming arrows of the evil one. Take the helmet of salvation and the sword of the Spirit, which is the word of God.

Ephesians 6:10–17

Man does not live on bread alone but on every word that comes from the mouth of the LORD.

Deuteronomy 8:3

Deuteronomy 8:3—Words for the Devil

When tempted by Satan (Luke 4:1–13), Jesus responded with three separate quotations from Deuteronomy: 8:3, 6:13, and 6:16. In the desert, Israelites had learned that God would provide all they needed. Jesus, also in the desert, quoted Scripture to forcefully remind Satan of that lesson.

Devotional Thought on
TEMPTATION

How can we overcome temptation (whether it's to spend too much money, get sexually involved, cheat at school, eat too much, or go where we shouldn't)? Answer: By following the example of Jesus.

Led into the wilderness, the Son of God was subjected to a variety of temptations. And each time Christ resisted enticements to sin by quoting Scripture. Finally he said "'Away from me, Satan! For it is written: "Worship the Lord your God, and serve him only."'" "Then the devil left him, and angels came and attended him" (Matthew 4:10–11).

Jesus quoted Scripture as a defense against temptation. Regardless of feelings or circumstances, he kept coming back to the fact of God's Word. Every time the tempter opened his mouth, Jesus responded, "It is written."

That's a good example to follow—quoting Bible verses in the heat of spiritual battles. So memorize a couple of verses today that deal with the specific temptations you face.

God's Words of Life on
TRUST

Trust in the LORD with all your heart and lean not on your own understanding; in all your ways acknowledge him, and he will make your paths staight.

Proverbs 3:5-6

Those who know your name will trust in you, for you, LORD, have never forsaken those who seek you.

Psalm 9:10

Blessed is the man who trusts in the LORD, whose confidence is in him.

Jeremiah 17:7

They brought Daniel and threw him into the lions' den. And when Daniel was lifted from the den, no wound was found on him, because he had trusted in his God.

Daniel 6:16, 23

Trust in the LORD forever, for the LORD, the LORD, is the Rock eternal.

Isaiah 26:4

Furious with rage, Nebuchadnezzar summoned Shadrach, Meshach and Abednego. So these men were brought before the king, and Nebuchadnezzar said to them, "Is it true, Shadrach, Meshach and Abednego, that you do not serve my gods or worship the image of gold I have set up? Now if you are ready to fall down and worship the image I made, very good. But if you do not worship it, you will be thrown immediately into a blazing furnace. Then what god will be able to rescue you from my hand?" Shadrach, Meshach and Abednego replied to the king, "O Nebuchadnezzar, we do not need to defend ourselves before you in this matter. If we are thrown into the blazing furnace, the God we serve is able to save us from it, and he will rescue us from your hand, O king."

Daniel 3:13–17

This is what the Sovereign LORD, the Holy One of Israel, says: "In repentance and rest is your salvation, in quietness and trust is your strength."

Isaiah 30:15

If you confess with your mouth, "Jesus is Lord," and believe in your heart that God raised him from the dead, you will be saved. For it is with your heart that you believe and are justified, and it is with your mouth that you confess and are saved. As the Scripture says, "Anyone who trusts in him will never be put to shame."

Romans 10:9–11

God's Words of Life on
TRUST

Jesus said, "Trust in God; trust also in me."

John 14:1

This is what the LORD says: "Cursed is the one who trusts in man, who depends on flesh for his strength and whose heart turns away from the LORD. He will be like a bush in the wastelands; he will not see prosperity when it comes. He will dwell in the parched places of the desert, in a salt land where no one lives. But blessed is the man who trusts in the LORD, whose confidence is in him. He will be like a tree planted by the water that sends out its roots by the stream. It does not fear when heat comes; its leaves are always green. It has no worries in a year of drought and never fails to bear fruit."

Jeremiah 17:5–8

Jeremiah 17:6—Whom to Trust?

Buy two identical plants in a nursery. Plant one in a desert, and one by a river. For a few days they'll look alike, but what happens after a few weeks? That's the image Jeremiah uses. The person who trusts in human beings will end up like a shriveled bush (Jeremiah 17:6), while the person who trusts God will be like a tree that has its roots sunk deep beside a stream (Jeremiah 17:8).

Devotional Thought on
TRUST

Married people make it their business to remember how love began. Anniversaries recall their wedding day, year after year. Wedding rings remind them of their commitment. Wedding photos capture the moment when "two become one." In remembering the beginning of their love, couples often find new hope for the future.

The book of Psalms remembers too. When things get bad, these poems often refer to the past—particularly to the great events when, under Moses, the Israelite nation began. God freed the Israelites from Egyptian slavery, carried them through the Red Sea, gave them directions for living, and ushered them into the promised land.

The historical psalms (77, 78, 105, 106) invite us, along with the Israelites, to relive history. Like married couples remembering back, we can recall God's work—his powerful victories recorded all through Scripture, his promises and proofs of love toward his people. And we can refer to God's history with us as individuals, too. Who cannot count some blessings, some undeserved favors? Through such remembering we are strengthened to face the future, and to recommit ourselves to trusting God's care.

199

God's Words of Life on
WISDOM

God appeared to Solomon and said to him,
"Ask for whatever you want me to give you."
Solomon answered God, "You have shown great
kindness to David my father and have made me
king in his place. Now, LORD God, let your
promise to my father David be confirmed, for
you have made me king over a people who are
as numerous as the dust of the earth. Give me
wisdom and knowledge, that I may lead this
people, for who is able to govern this great people of yours?" God said to Solomon, "Since this
is your heart's desire and you have not asked
for wealth, riches or honor, nor for the death of
your enemies, and since you have not asked for
a long life but for wisdom and knowledge to
govern my people over whom I have made you
king, therefore wisdom and knowledge will be
given you. And I will also give you wealth, riches
and honor, such as no king who was before you
ever had and none after you will have."

2 Chronicles 1:7–12

If any of you lacks wisdom, he should ask God,
who gives generously to all without finding
fault, and it will be given to him.

James 1:5

The fear of the LORD is the beginning of wisdom.

Psalm 111:10

Trust in the LORD with all your heart and lean not on your own understanding; in all your ways acknowledge him, and he will make your paths straight.

Proverbs 3:5-6

The mouth of the righteous man utters wisdom, and his tongue speaks what is just.

Psalm 37:30

Blessed is the man who finds wisdom, the man who gains understanding, for she is more profitable than silver and yields better returns than gold. She is more precious than rubies; nothing you desire can compare with her. Long life is in her right hand; in her left hand are riches and honor. Her ways are pleasant ways, and all her paths are peace. She is a tree of life to those who embrace her; those who lay hold of her will be blessed.

Proverbs 3:13–18

He who walks with the wise grows wise, but a companion of fools suffers harm.

Proverbs 13:20

Christ Jesus has become for us wisdom from God.

1 Corinthians 1:30

God's Words of Life on
WISDOM

My son, if you accept my words and store up my commands within you, turning your ear to wisdom and applying your heart to understanding, and if you call out for insight and cry aloud for understanding, and if you look for it as for silver and search for it as for hidden treasure, then you will understand the fear of the LORD and find the knowledge of God.

Proverbs 2:1–5

Wisdom is supreme; therefore get wisdom. Though it cost all you have, get understanding.

Proverbs 4:7

Proverbs 4:7—A Lifelong Quest

A father's advice can easily degenerate into, "Don't do this, don't do that." But the fatherly advice of Proverbs isn't preoccupied with rules. Instead, this father tries to help his son develop a love for the best things in life—just as his father did for him. This love for the best—and most of all for wisdom—begins with listening to your father's advice, but it goes beyond taking instructions. The love of wisdom becomes a lifelong quest that may make you wiser than your father.

Proverbs judges every thought or action by one standard: "Is this wise?" The word *wisdom* brings up pictures of gray-haired old men muttering obscure philosophic maxims. But that is almost the opposite of what Proverbs means by the word. Wisdom is above all practical and down to earth. Young people as well as old can and should have it. Wisdom teaches you how to live. It combines understanding with discipline—the kind of discipline an athlete needs in training. It also adds a healthy dose of good common sense—except that common sense isn't, and never has been, common.

How do you become a wise person? You must first begin to listen. Wisdom is freely available to those who will stop talking and start paying attention—to God and his Word, to parents, to wise counselors. Anybody can become wise, Proverbs says. Wisdom is not reserved for a brainy elite. But becoming wise requires self-discipline to study and humbly seek wisdom at every opportunity.

God's Words of Life on
WORK

Jesus said, "My Father is always at his work to this very day, and I, too, am working."

John 5:17

The LORD God took the man and put him in the Garden of Eden to work it and take care of it.

Genesis 2:15

It is good and proper for a man to eat and drink, and to find satisfaction in his toilsome labor under the sun during the few days of life God has given him—for this is his lot. Moreover, when God gives any man wealth and possessions, and enables him to enjoy them, to accept his lot and be happy in his work— this is a gift of God.

Ecclesiastes 5:18–19

In the name of the Lord Jesus Christ, we command you, brothers, to keep away from every brother who is idle and does not live according to the teaching you received from us. For you yourselves know how you ought to follow our example. We were not idle when we were with you, nor did we eat anyone's food without paying for it. On the contrary, we worked night and day, laboring and toiling so that we would not be a burden to any of you. We did this, not because we do not have the right to such help, but in order to make ourselves a model for you to follow. For even when we were with you, we gave you this rule: "If a man will not work, he shall not eat."

2 Thessalonians 3:6–10

Lazy hands make a man poor, but diligent hands bring wealth.

Proverbs 10:4

If a man is lazy, the rafters sag; if his hands are idle, the house leaks.

Ecclesiastes 10:18

Jesus said, "Take my yoke upon you and learn from me, for I am gentle and humble in heart, and you will find rest for your souls. For my yoke is easy and my burden is light."

Matthew 11:29–30

Anyone who enters God's rest also rests from his own work, just as God did from his.

Hebrews 4:10

Remember the Sabbath day by keeping it holy. Six days you shall labor and do all your work, but the seventh day is a Sabbath to the LORD your God. On it you shall not do any work, neither you, nor your son or daughter, nor your manservant or maidservant, nor your animals, nor the alien within your gates. For in six days the LORD made the heavens and the earth, the sea, and all that is in them, but he rested on the seventh day.

Exodus 20:8–11

God blessed the seventh day and made it holy, because on it he rested from all the work of creating that he had done.

Genesis 2:3

Genesis 2:3—God at Work

As Michelangelo knew very well, his work was a poor, dim image of what God had created. Over the plaster vault of the Sistine Chapel rose the immense dome of God's sky, breathtaking in its simple beauty. Mountains, seas, the continents—all these, and much more, are the creative work of God, the Master Artist. Author Eugene Peterson has written, "The Bible begins with the announcement, 'In the beginning God created,' not 'sat majestic in the heavens' and not 'was filled with beauty and love.' He created. He did something." In the beginning, God went to work.

Devotional Thought on
WORK

Y ou don't have to be a pastor or a mis-
sionary to be in "full-time Christian service." Any Christian can do that. A clerk at
McDonald's can be a full-time Christian. A
housewife can dedicate herself completely to
serving God. A high school or college student
can be a full-time Christian, too.

What is a full-time Christian?

A full-time Christian is someone who real-
izes that their relationship with Jesus is the
most important thing about them—more
important than how rich they are or how they
look or how talented they are, more important than how successful they'll be in their
career or how well-known their family is.

A full-time Christian is someone who's
willing to let God use them any way he sees
fit—to just live the kind of life that people
admire for its consistency and strength and
honesty, to tell those around them about
Jesus, or to be the kind of helpful, supporting
friend that people come to when they have
problems. Or for that matter, to go to Africa
to spread the gospel, if that's what God
wants.

Other titles to enjoy in the
God's Words of Life Series include:

*God's Words of Life from
the Classics Devotional Bible*

*God's Words of Life from
the Women's Devotional Bible*

*God's Words of Life from
the Men's Devotional Bible*

We have a gift for inspiration™